HEALTHCARE AND YOUR RIGHTS UNDER THE LAW

by
Margaret C. Jasper

Oceana's Legal Almanac Series:
Law for the Layperson

2002
Oceana Publications, Inc.
Dobbs Ferry, New York

Library of Congress Control Number: 2002112335

ISBN: 0-379-11371-6

Oceana's Legal Almanac Series: Law for the Layperson
ISSN 1075-7376

Manufactured in the United States of America on acid-free paper.

To My Husband Chris

Your love and support
are my motivation and inspiration

-and-

In memory of my son, Jimmy

Table of Contents

CHAPTER 3: HOSPITALS AND NURSING HOMES

CHAPTER 4:
MEDICAL RECORDS: ACCESS AND PRIVACY ISSUES

CHAPTER 5:
PRIVATE HEALTH INSURANCE

CHAPTER 6:
THE CONSOLIDATED OMNIBUS BUDGET RECONCILIATION ACT (COBRA)

ABOUT THE AUTHOR

MARGARET C. JASPER is an attorney engaged in the general practice of law in South Salem, New York, concentrating in the areas of personal injury and entertainment law. Ms. Jasper holds a Juris Doctor degree from Pace University School of Law, White Plains, New York, is a member of the New York and Connecticut bars, and is certified to practice before the United States District Courts for the Southern and Eastern Districts of New York, the United States Court of Appeals for the Second Circuit, and the United States Supreme Court.

Ms. Jasper has been appointed to the panel of arbitrators of the American Arbitration Association and the law guardian panel for the Family Court of the State of New York, is a member of the Association of Trial Lawyers of America, and is a New York State licensed real estate broker and member of the Westchester County Board of Realtors, operating as Jasper Real Estate, in South Salem, New York. Margaret Jasper maintains a website at http://members.aol.com/JasperLaw.

Ms. Jasper is the author and general editor of the following legal almanacs: Juvenile Justice and Children's Law; Marriage and Divorce; Estate Planning; The Law of Contracts; The Law of Dispute Resolution; Law for the Small Business Owner; The Law of Personal Injury; Real Estate Law for the Homeowner and Broker; Everyday Legal Forms; Dictionary of Selected Legal Terms; The Law of Medical Malpractice; The Law of Product Liability; The Law of No-Fault Insurance; The Law of Immigration; The Law of Libel and Slander; The Law of Buying and Selling; Elder Law; The Right to Die; AIDS Law; The Law of Obscenity and Pornography; The Law of Child Custody; The Law of Debt Collection; Consumer Rights Law; Bankruptcy Law for the Individual Debtor; Victim's Rights Law; Animal Rights Law; Workers' Compensation Law; Employee Rights in the Workplace; Probate Law; Environmental Law; Labor Law; The Americans with Disabilities Act; The Law of Capital Punishment; Education Law; The Law of Violence Against Women; Landlord-Tenant

Law; Insurance Law; Religion and the Law; Commercial Law; Motor Vehicle Law; Social Security Law; The Law of Drunk Driving; The Law of Speech and the First Amendment; Employment Discrimination Under Title VII; Hospital Liability Law; Home Mortgage Law Primer; Copyright Law; Patent Law; Trademark Law; Special Education Law; The Law of Attachment and Garnishment; Banks and their Customers; Credit Cards and the Law; Identity Theft and How To Protect Yourself; Welfare: Your Rights and the Law; Individual Bankruptcy and Restructuring; Harassment in the Workplace; and Health Care and Your Rights.

INTRODUCTION

One of an individual's most important goals is to maintain good health, and obtain the best health care available for themselves and their families. This remains an important objective throughout one's life. One way to achieve this goal is to familiarize oneself with all of the health care rights available under the law. This almanac is designed to assist the reader in understanding those rights.

This almanac discusses the individual's right to make informed decisions about their health care, including their right to treatment, as well as their right to refuse treatment. An individual is also entitled to be informed about every aspect of their care, including the risks and benefits of proposed treatment plans and medications, and the results of any testing procedures.

An individual is also entitled to research the background and credentials of prospective health care providers, including physicians, hospitals, nursing homes, and other health care facilities and providers. This almanac provides information on obtaining this information.

The individual's right to privacy of their medical information is also examined, including the special circumstances under which that right may be limited, such as situations involving the mandatory disclosure of HIV/AIDS test results.

This almanac also discusses an individual's rights under health insurance plans, including the procedures for resolving billing disputes, and appealing adverse coverage decisions. Government access to health care coverage for children and low-income families is also explored, as well as the senior citizen's rights to health care coverage under Medicare.

This almanac also sets forth a terminated employee's right to continue coverage under a group health insurance plan pursuant to the provisions of the Consolidated Omnibus Budget Reconciliation Act (COBRA) of 1986.

The Appendix provides resource directories, applicable statutes, and other pertinent information and data. The Glossary contains definitions of many of the terms used throughout the almanac.

CHAPTER 1:
CHECKING THE CREDENTIALS OF YOUR HEALTH CARE PROVIDERS

IN GENERAL

Finding good medical care is a serious matter. However, all too often, consumers do not investigate the background of their health care providers before undergoing treatment. There have been many disturbing reports of substandard medical care by physicians and hospitals. The consumer is entitled to access this information so that they can make an informed decision about the physicians and other health care professionals they select to care for them and their loved ones.

Consumers have the right to receive accurate, easily understood information about their prospective physicians. Such information should include the following:

1. The physician's education, board certification, and recertification status.
2. The names of all hospitals where the physician has admitting privileges.
3. The number of years the physician has been in practice, and the number of years as a specialist if so designated.
4. The physician's experience with performing certain medical or surgical procedures.
5. The physician's consumer satisfaction measures.
6. The physician's clinical quality performance measures.
7. The physician's service performance measures.
8. The physician's accreditation status.
9. The corporate form of the physician's practice—i.e., ownership and management, sole proprietorship or group practice, etc.

10. The availability of translation or interpretation services for non-English speakers and people with communication disabilities.

11. Any cancellation, suspension, or exclusion from participation in Federal programs or sanctions from Federal agencies; any suspension or revocation of medical licensure, Federal controlled substance license, or hospital privileges.

This chapter provides information on researching the credentials of health care providers, including physicians, hospitals, and other medical facilities.

SOURCES OF INFORMATION

The American Medical Association provides background and credentialing information for physicians on-line at *http://www.ama-assn.org*. You can find out where your prospective doctor went to medical school, whether or not they are board-certified, as well as their office address and phone number. In addition, the American Board of Medical Specialties operates a website at *http://www.abms.org*, where you can find out if a specific physician has been certified as a specialist by one of their specialty boards.

The Federation of State Medical Boards operates a website at *http://www.fsmb.org*, which has direct links to all of the state medical licensing boards. You can access your state's medical board to find out the status of a doctor's license, and whether he or she has ever been the subject of disciplinary procedures. Several states now also include medical malpractice and hospital disciplinary action information on their own websites.

A Directory of State Physician Licensing Bureaus is set forth at Appendix 1.

Another service which provides comprehensive background information on health care providers nationwide is KnowX, which is available on-line at *http://www.knowx.com*. For a relatively small fee, the consumer can access information concerning a health care provider's location, credentials, license verification and disciplinary actions. The KnowX service includes information on medical doctors (MDs), as well as doctors of osteopathy (Dos), and doctors of chiropractic (Dcs), with active licenses to practice in the United States. KnowX also contains a database which lists court information, enabling the consumer to find out whether any lawsuits or judgments have been filed against a particular doctor.

The County Clerk's Office in a particular jurisdiction generally provides public access to its database of legal actions filed in the jurisdiction. It is possible to research whether a particular doctor, hospital, or other health care provider or medical facility is the defendant in any recently filed lawsuits, and even review copies of the litigation papers, such as the actual complaint, which are on file with the Clerk's office.

There are also a number of private companies who specialize in checking the background of health care providers. Health Care Choices is a New York not-for-profit corporation dedicated to educating the public about the nation's health care system. HealthGrades.com, Inc. is a private company that provides "report cards" on doctors, hospitals, health plans and nursing homes.

PROFILING LAWS

In an effort to improve access to information concerning the credentials of health care providers, a number of states have passed profiling laws. Some states, such as California and Massachusetts, provide malpractice information to the public as a result of a requirement included in profiling legislation. Profiling laws require state agencies to compile practice information on physicians and other practitioners from various sources and then publish the resulting profile on the internet. Profiles generally include information such as the practitioner's education and training, specialty, hospital affiliations, disciplinary actions, closed malpractice cases and hospital disciplinary proceedings.

There is variation among states with respect to penalties imposed on practitioners for failing to report or for reporting inaccurate information. For example, Idaho assesses a $50/day fine for the period a practitioner is not in compliance with the statutory reporting requirements. In Florida, failure to comply with the profiling statute can subject the practitioner to disciplinary action including failure to have a license renewed.

THE JOINT COMMISSION ON ACCREDITATION OF HEALTHCARE ORGANIZATIONS (JCAHO)

The Joint Commission on Accreditation of Healthcare Organizations (JCAHO) is the nation's predominant standards-setting and accrediting body in health care and evaluates and accredits nearly 19,000 health care organizations and programs in the United States. The JCAHO was founded in 1951 as an independent, not-for-profit organization. The mission of the JCAHO is to continuously improve the safety and quality of care provided to the public through the provision of health care accreditation and related services that support performance improvement in health care organizations. The JCAHO also sponsors a variety of education programs and provides relevant publications for health care professionals.

The JCAHO evaluation and accreditation services are provided for the following types of organizations:

1. General, psychiatric, children's and rehabilitation hospitals.

2. Health care networks, including health plans, integrated delivery networks and preferred provider organizations.

3. Home care organizations, including those that provide home health services, personal care and support services, home infusion and other pharmacy services, durable medical equipment services and hospice services.

4. Nursing homes and other long term care facilities, including subacute care programs, dementia programs and long term care pharmacies.

5. Assisted Living residences that provide or coordinate personal services, 24-hour supervision and assistance, activities and health-related services.

6. Behavioral health care organizations, including those that provide mental health, chemical dependency, and mental retardation/developmental disabilities services for patients of various ages in various organized service settings; and managed behavioral health care organizations.

7. Ambulatory care providers, including outpatient surgery facilities, rehabilitation centers, infusion centers, group practices and others.

8. Clinical laboratories.

Accreditation by the JCAHO is recognized nationwide as a symbol of quality that indicates that an organization meets certain performance standards. The JCAHO's standards address the organization's level of performance in key functional areas, such as patient rights. The JCAHO develops its standards in consultation with health care experts, providers, measurement experts, purchasers and consumers. To earn and maintain accreditation, an organization must undergo an on-site survey by a JCAHO survey team at least every three years. Laboratories must be surveyed every two years.

The JCAHO is governed by a 28-member Board of Commissioners, which includes nurses, physicians, consumers, medical directors, administrators, providers, employers, labor representatives, health plan leaders, quality experts, ethicists, health insurance administrators and educators. Its corporate members are the American College of Physicians; the American College of Surgeons; the American Dental Association; the American Hospital Association; and the American Medical Association. More than 650 physicians, nurses, health care administrators, medical technologists, psychologists, respiratory therapists, pharmacists, durable medical equipment providers and social workers are employed by the JCAHO to conduct accreditation surveys.

The JCAHO also publishes "Quality Check"—a comprehensive internet guide to accredited organizations, where a consumer can search for quality information on their local hospital. Quality Check provides a list of nearly 20,000 JCAHO-accredited health care organizations and programs throughout the United States and includes each organization's name, address, telephone number, accreditation decision, accreditation date, and current accreditation status and effective date.

In addition, for more in-depth quality information, consumers can check the individual performance reports available for many accredited organizations. Performance reports provide detailed information about an organization's performance and how it compares to similar organizations.

Hospitals are required by law to maintain a statistical record on all procedures performed in the hospital. The consumer can request this information. The consumer may also inquire about the credentials of the hospital's staff, including their nurses and others associated with the prospective patient's daily care.

A Directory of State Licensing Agencies for Medical Facilities is set forth at Appendix 2.

CHAPTER 2: THE PATIENT'S RIGHT TO PARTICIPATE IN HEALTH CARE DECISIONS

IN GENERAL

Patients have the right and responsibility to fully participate in all decisions related to their health care. If they are unable to fully participate in their treatment decisions, they have the right to be represented by parents, guardians, family members, or other conservators.

In order to ensure the consumer's right and ability to participate in treatment decisions, health care professionals should:

1. Provide patients with easily understood information and opportunity to decide among treatment options consistent with the informed consent process.

2. Discuss all treatment options with a patient in a culturally competent manner, including the option of no treatment at all.

3. Ensure that persons with disabilities have effective communications with members of the health system in making such decisions.

4. Discuss all current treatments a consumer may be undergoing, including those alternative treatments that are self-administered.

5. Discuss all risks, benefits, and consequences to treatment or nontreatment.

6. Give patients the opportunity to refuse treatment and to express preferences about future treatment decisions.

7. Discuss the use of advance directives—both living wills and durable powers of attorney for health care—with patients and their designated family members.

8. Abide by the decisions made by their patients and/or their designated representatives consistent with the informed consent process.

INFORMED CONSENT

A patient gives consent to medical treatment either by (1) express consent or (2) implied consent.

Express Consent

Express consent is obtained either in writing or orally. The health care provider is required to fully disclose all of the known and significant facts relevant to the procedure, in layperson's language, so that the patient can make an intelligent decision as to whether to go forward with the treatment. The following information should be provided to the patient to satisfy the informed consent requirement:

1. The diagnosis of the patient's condition and the prognosis without the proposed treatment;

2. The nature of the proposed treatment;

3. The goal to be achieved by the proposed treatment and the chance that the treatment will be successful;

4. The risks of the proposed treatment;

5. Any alternative treatments to the proposed treatment;

6. Identify:

    (a) The health care provider(s) who discussed the proposed treatment with the patient;

    (b) The health care provider(s) who will perform the proposed treatment;

7. Obtain consent to deviate from the proposed treatment in case of unforeseen circumstances.

8. Obtain consent to dispose of any tissue, organs or other body parts, if needed, for pathological study or research;

9. Acknowledgement that the patient's questions were fully discussed and adequately answered.

10. The patient's and/or legal guardian's signature, the signature of a witness, and the date, time, and location that the consent form was signed. If the patient is a minor, the parents may consent to the procedure, or, in the case of divorce, it is usually the parent having legal custody who may consent.

Where the health care provider has failed to obtain such consent, or where the quality of the consent is challenged, the patient may claim lack of informed consent for the procedure.

A sample informed consent agreement is set forth at Appendix 3.

Implied Consent

Implied consent is obtained, for example, when a patient submits to a *simple* procedure. However, there is no implied consent where the procedure is invasive or non-customary.

Further, once a surgeon begins an internal surgical procedure, there is a presumption of implied consent if the surgeon does other *necessary* procedures in the process. This is so even if there are relatives in the vicinity because the surgeon is not permitted to leave the operating room, once the surgery has begun, to obtain consent.

However, such implied consent only applies to necessary procedures. If the procedure is elective, the surgeon has the duty to delay until he receives the necessary consent for the additional surgery.

Implied consent also applies in emergency situations. If the emergency involves risk to the patient's life, or the patient is unable to give consent due to unconsciousness, coma or other incompetence, it has been held that the patient would have consented to the treatment if he or she were able, thus consent is implied in such situations.

The existence of the emergency should be entered into the medical records, including the reason why the procedure was necessary, e.g., the patient's airway was blocked and an emergency tracheotomy was necessary or the patient would have choked to death.

Lack of Informed Consent

Lack of informed consent means that the patient did not fully understand what the health care provider was going to do, and was injured as a result of the health care provider's action. Further, the patient claims that if he had known what the health care provider planned to do, the patient would not have consented and, therefore, would have avoided the injury.

Absent an emergency, if the health care provider is able to ascertain, in advance of a surgical procedure, all of the possible alternatives available if an unexpected situation should arise during the operation, the patient should be informed of the alternatives and given the chance to decide if those alternatives are acceptable before the health care provider proceeds with the procedure.

Prescription Drugs

More often than not, a patient is prescribed medication without any details given to them about the particular medication. They simply take the often illegibly handwritten prescription to the pharmacy, have it filled, and start taking the drug according to the label's directions. However, patients have the right to know much more about the medicines that they are taking, and should take advantage of those rights.

Most problems associated with prescription drugs occur because the patient did not receive enough information concerning the medicine to use it properly. For example, they are unaware of what side effects to expect, or they improperly mix the medication with a food or drink, or another medication. The improper use of prescription medications can be deadly.

It is important to ask your medical provider every question you may have concerning a medication that is prescribed for you. A patient has the right to be informed about all aspects of their medical treatment, including the risks and benefits of the medicines prescribed; the potential side effects; and the necessity of monitoring the medication's effects. The patient also has the right to know the results of any tests which demonstrate whether or not the medication is working. For example, if the medical provider prescribes a cholesterol-reducing drug, the patient should be advised whether or not the medication is effectively reducing their cholesterol level.

The patient should also discuss with their medical provider all of the medicines that they are presently taking, including over-the-counter medicines, and whether there are any concerns about the interaction between those medicines with the medicine being prescribed. In particular, a patient has the right to the following information:

1. The name of the medicine and how it is intended to treat the patient's condition;

2. The dosage, frequency and duration prescribed, and whether there are refills available;

3. The foods, drinks, and other medicines that may negatively interact with the medication being prescribed.

4. The potential side effects of the medicine, and instructions on how to proceed should the patient experience those side effects;

5. An explanation of any terms or directions the patient does not understand.

6. A copy of any written information that may be available concerning the medication they are being prescribed.

The Food and Drug Administration (FDA) provides updated information about medication errors, including specific drugs that have been confused with one another. The information has been compiled based on voluntary reports received from consumers, doctors and other clinicians, as well as mandatory reports from manufacturers. Information concerning medication errors is available from the FDA on-line at *http://www.fda.gov.*

Blood and Blood Products Safety

The blood supply plays a critical role in the American health care system. Each year approximately 14 million units of blood are drawn from volunteer donors for use by more than 3.5 million Americans. In addition to providing life-sustaining blood components, such as red blood cells and platelets, much of this blood, and an additional 12 million units of plasma, is processed into further products, such as immune globulin, albumin and clotting factors such as anti-hemophilic factor.

While blood and blood products can be lifesaving products for millions of Americans, blood products carry the risk of transmission of undetected infectious disease. Patients who have received blood transfusions or blood products have the right to know t6

hat these products are safe. As set forth below, the Department of Health and Human Services (HHS), along with other federal agencies, have implemented certain programs to notify recipients when a problem is detected.

Patient Notification System

In 1998, the blood industry started the Patient Notification System, a voluntary system to inform recipients when certain blood-derived products, such as clotting factors, are withdrawn or recalled. The system allows registered individuals to receive notifications by telephone, express mail, fax or e-mail.

To date, the voluntary program has registered fewer than 10 percent of eligible patients, health care providers and distributors. In 1999, the Food and Drug Administration (FDA) announced its intent to issue regulations on tracking certain plasma derivatives and notifying users of withdrawals and recalls. The FDA solicited public comment and is now drafting proposed regulations.

The Hepatitis C "Lookback" Program

The Centers for Disease Control (CDC) estimates there are approximately 3 million Americans chronically infected with the hepatitis C virus (HCV), including about 300,000 who were infected by blood transfusions prior to 1992. Many Americans with HCV are unaware they have the disease because it does not cause symptoms until it is far advanced.

In 1998, a "lookback" program was established to notify people who received blood in the past from a potentially infected donor of the potential risk and the need to get tested. Based on guidance from the FDA, blood establishments have been identifying affected units and notifying hospital transfusion centers so that blood recipients can be traced. More information about the HCV "lookback" program is available from the CDC's Hepatitis Resource Center available on-line at *http://www.cdc.gov/hepatitis*.

THE PATIENT'S RIGHT TO REFUSE TREATMENT

Most states acknowledge that a competent adult has the legal right to refuse medical care. On the other hand, many states also set forth certain policy concerns—such as preservation of life and suicide prevention—to limit this right. The courts have looked to the circumstances concerning the patient when denial of the patient's rights are put in issue.

Generally, if the patient is capable of recovery, the state's interest in preserving life has more merit than when the patient is on his or her death bed with no possibility of recovery. Further, the courts have distinguished between the act of suicide and the patient's right to die a natural death without being placed on life support.

States have also expressed concern over the impact refusal of medical treatment will have on innocent third parties—in particular, minor children. For example, if the refusal to have a critical blood transfusion will cause a single mother to die and leave her children orphaned, the court will likely order the parent to undergo the treatment. The court will also usually order a pregnant woman to undergo treatment which is necessary to protect the unborn child.

A health care provider—e.g., on moral grounds—may not be able to accept the patient's wishes to forego necessary treatment. In that case, the health care provider should assist the patient in locating a health care provider who is able to care for the patient according to his or her wishes.

Some health care providers have raised concerns that withholding treatment is tantamount to abandonment. However, the courts have generally held that where treatment would be futile, terminating or withholding treatment is not abandonment.

Minors

Minors are incompetent to make decisions concerning their right to forego medical treatment. The minor's parents make the decisions on the minor's behalf. However, when a minor is in critical need of treatment but the parent—e.g., due to religious beliefs—will not consent, court orders are routinely granted to the health care provider to administer the treatment. In some cases, a guardian is appointed by the court to protect the child.

A health care provider who is faced with a life-threatening situation must render the necessary treatment to the minor despite the parent's wishes, and instruct the parents to obtain a court order immediately if they want to prevent such treatment.

In situations where the minor is in such a physical state that any attempt to sustain life would be futile and cruel, the courts have held that the parents and health care provider can mutually decide to withhold treatment without seeking a court order. Nevertheless, this law generally does not permit the withholding of food and water as a means to hasten death in the case of a minor.

Religious Beliefs

Certain religious groups hold that medical treatment—e.g., blood transfusions—violates their religious beliefs. In these cases, the courts have generally held that a competent adult, without dependent children, may refuse treatment. However, as previously discussed, where there is an overriding state concern, such as the protection of third parties, the adult may be compelled to accept the treatment.

Release from Liability

Most hospitals will require a patient, or his or her representative, to sign a document which releases the attending physician, the hospital and its employees from liability if treatment is withheld or withdrawn. The document generally states the circumstances of the patient's condition, e.g., brain death, etc., giving rise to the request to terminate treatment.

As set forth below, the release of liability document also references the patient's living will and durable power of attorney for health care as proof of the patient's desire to forego life sustaining procedures and his or her appointment of an agent to make this decision if he or she is unable to do so.

In a subsequent medical malpractice action, a defendant may set forth a defense alleging that the patient assumed the risk of non-treatment by virtue of the release of liability. However, the release would not limit the health care provider's liability for negligence. If the release contained such a provision, it would likely be unenforceable on public policy grounds.

A sample release from liability is set forth at Appendix 4.

ADVANCE DIRECTIVES

Advance directives are the instructions one prepares in order to designate his or her wishes concerning end-of-life health care treatment. Executing an advance directive gives an individual the opportunity to make his or her own health care decisions long after he or she has lost the capacity to do so. The opportunity to execute advance directives responds to the individual's wishes to have some control over his or her destiny. Advance directives respond to the individual's fear that medical technology will prolong their life long after any reasonable possibility of recovery has disappeared.

Many people prefer to "die with dignity" rather than remain comatose in a hospital bed attached to life support equipment for an indefinite duration. Further, the emotional toll that such a scenario causes the patient's family is another important factor to be considered. An advance directive authorizes the medical care provider to cease some or all of these life support measures. On the other hand, an advance directive may also be used to instruct the medical care provider to undertake certain life-sustaining treatments in certain defined circumstances. In short, it is about giving the patient the choice and the right to make these decisions.

In general, there are two types of advance directives: (1) A Living Will; and (2) A Durable Power of Attorney for Health Care. However, if you execute both a Living Will and a Durable Power of Attorney for Health Care, you must make sure that the terms of both documents are consistent to avoid confusion or invalidation. Discuss this matter with your physician and provide a copy of your documents.

It is important to check with your hospital to make sure your documents conform to their requirements. If your physician, or your hospital, appear to be unwilling to comply with your wishes, you should consider finding alternative medical care.

Discuss this matter with your family, so that they will be prepared if called on to support your decision. Provide copies of your living will and durable power of attorney documents to your family and your minister, rabbi, or other religious advisor. Do not keep your living will or power of attorney in a place where they will not be easily found. You must make your wishes known ahead of time to ensure that they will be followed. An advance directive may be amended or revoked at the will of the individual executing the directive.

All 50 states and the District of Columbia have laws recognizing the use of advance directives. The availability and scope of one or both advance directives varies from state to state, therefore, the reader is advised to check the law of his or her jurisdiction for specific provisions.

The Living Will

A living will is a written declaration, directed to your physician, stating that you wish to forgo extraordinary treatment of a terminal illness, in order to die a natural death. Although living wills may not be statutorily recognized in all states, the majority of states have enacted "right to die" legislation. Further, an individual has a constitutional right to execute a living will.

The purpose of right-to-die legislation is to give a person some say over the manner in which they will be treated should they develop an incurable illness or enter a persistent vegetative state, and become unable to communicate their wishes at that time.

A living will provides family and loved ones some guidance in making a very painful decision. It also allows health care providers to withdraw or withhold life-support treatment without risking a medical malpractice lawsuit. Generally, a living will provides that no heroic measures should be taken to prolong the individual's life where there is no reasonable expectation of recovery. However, pain medication is still usually administered.

A sample Living Will is set forth at Appendix 5.

Requirements

There are certain requirements that must be met to ensure recognition of a living will, and some states require the use of a statutory form for a living will to be valid. Although state laws vary, right to die statutes generally require that there be two witnesses to the maker's signature, neither of whom can be related to the maker or beneficiaries of his or her estate. In addition, two physicians must diagnose the patient as terminally ill. Many states also provide that a living will is valid only if signed after the physician has informed the patient that he or she has an incurable illness. Before executing a living will, it is prudent to determine exactly what requirements are imposed in your state.

A table of state Living Will statutes is set forth at Appendix 6.

Durable Power of Attorney for Health Care

In order to have your wishes concerning medical treatment known and honored should you become incapacitated, you can designate a health care agent by executing what is generally known as a Durable Power of Attorney for Health Care, also known as a Health Care Proxy in some jurisdictions. In effect, the person you appoint "stands in your shoes" for the purposes of making your health care decisions.

You can specify the type of treatment you desire, as well as the type of treatment you do not want. For example, you can instruct your "attorney-in-fact" to either require or prohibit the use of life-support systems should you be diagnosed with a terminal illness, or you can leave that decision in his or her hands.

A sample Durable Power of Attorney for Health Care is set forth in the Appendix 7.

You can appoint an alternate agent to decide for you if your health care agent is not available or able to act when decisions must be made. Otherwise, health care providers will make treatment decisions for you that follow instructions you gave while you were still able to do so. Any instructions that you write on your Health Care Proxy form will guide health care providers under these circumstances.

Withdrawal of or Withholding Medical Treatment

An individual has a constitutional right to request the withdrawal or withholding of medical treatment, including the cessation of food and water, even if doing so will result in the person's death. Honoring a person's right to refuse medical treatment or other life sustaining intervention, especially at the end of life, is the most widely practiced and widely accepted right to die policy in our society.

Patients have the right to stop not only commonly recognized life support measures, such as respirators, but to also discontinue any other medical treatments that may prolong life, such as kidney dialysis, heart medication, antibiotics, blood transfusions, etc., regardless of whether the refusal may result in death. Nevertheless, the patient is also entitled to receive symptomatic treatment, such as pain medication, even if the pain medication has the effect of hastening their death.

Under the law, a health care provider cannot commence a medical procedure without first obtaining a patient's informed consent. Thus, a health care provider who imposes medical treatment contrary to the instructions left in an advance directive may be guilty of medical battery. Claims of battery against physicians for nonconsensual medical care have been recognized for some time even if the medical procedure is harmless, beneficial, or life-sustaining. The courts are becoming increasingly willing to find that battery has occurred in cases in which a health care provider refused to honor the directions left in an advance directive or given by an appointed agent.

The AMA Statement on Withholding or Withdrawing of Life-Prolonging Medical Treatment is set forth at Appendix 8.

The Cruzan Decision

The *Cruzan* case involved a petition brought by parents to remove life support from their daughter who was in a persistent vegetative state. The holding in *Cruzan* supports the desirability of individual choice in the formalization of advance directives.

In *Cruzan*, the Supreme Court held that:

1. Patients have the right to reject treatment, including life-sustaining treatment;

2. There is no distinction between artificial hydration and nutrition and any other form of treatment;

3. The distinction between "withholding" and "withdrawing" treatment is of no significance; and

4. The present incompetence of the patient is not an essential barrier to respecting the patient's wishes.

Nevertheless, the Supreme Court affirmed the individual state's right to set their own standards concerning evidence of an incompetent patient's wishes. By implication, this means that the state is not bound to honor the wishes of family members of the patient, but can set forth its own criteria to follow.

For example, the state may require: (1) an explicit statement by the patient as to his or her wishes concerning the withholding of certain treatment—i.e., the execution of a living will; or (2) the appointment by the patient of a proxy to make those decisions in the event of his or her incapacitation, i.e., the "durable power of attorney for health care.

In the *Cruzan* case, the State of Missouri required "clear and convincing evidence" that Ms. Cruzan wished to have life-sustaining treatment withheld, in this case tubal feeding.

The Supreme Court decision effectively permitted the State of Missouri to reject the petition brought by the parents. However, if Ms. Cruzan had executed advance directives which set forth her wishes to have treatment withheld, or if she had appointed a proxy to make those decisions on her behalf, the Supreme Court would have upheld her wishes according to her constitutional right.

Do Not Resuscitate Orders

A "do not resuscitate" order (DNR) refers to instructions given by the patient, or the patient's authorized representative, which generally provide that the patient does not want the medical staff to attempt cardiopulmonary resuscitation (CPR) in the event he or she suffers cardiac or respiratory arrest.

Prior to issuing a DNR order, the patient's attending physician must provide certain information to the patient, or to the surrogate, concerning the patient's condition, including:

1. The patient's diagnosis and prognosis;
2. The reasonably foreseeable risks and benefits of CPR; and
3. The consequences of a DNR order.

If the attending physician objects to the issuance of a DNR order, he or she must inform the patient or surrogate of that objection, and make arrangements to transfer the patient to another physician who will comply with the patient's directive.

A sample Do Not Resuscitate Order is set forth at Appendix 9.

THE PATIENT SELF-DETERMINATION ACT ("PSDA")

On November 5, 1990, the Patient Self-Determination Act (The "PSDA") was enacted. The PSDA became effective as of December 1, 1991. The purpose of the PSDA is to ensure that a patient maintains the right to control his or her own health care choices.

As established in the *Cruzan* case, discussed above, an individual has certain constitutionally protected rights concerning health care, such as the right to consent to, or refuse, treatment. The intent of the PSDA is to make sure patients are able to protect these rights in case they become at some point unable to do so. The Act requires health care facilities that receive Medicare and Medicaid funds to inform patients of their right to execute advance directives concerning their end-of-life care.

Requirements of the PSDA

As set forth below, there are three important provisions of the PSDA. They detail the obligations of:

1. Health care providers;
2. The individual states; and
3. The Secretary of Health and Human Services.

Health Care Providers

All hospitals, skilled nursing facilities, home health agencies, hospice programs and health maintenance organizations that participate in Medicare and Medicaid programs are required by the PSDA to:

1. Maintain written policies and procedures which ensure that every adult patient receives written information concerning advance directives, and their right to participate in the decisions affecting their health care;
2. Implement educational programs for the staff and the community on issues concerning advance directives; and
3. Document each patient's medical record concerning the existence of advance directives executed by the patient.

Health care providers are expressly prohibited from conditioning the provision of care, or from otherwise discriminating against the patient, based on whether or not the individual has executed an advance directive.

Under the PSDA, an advance directive refers to a written instruction executed by an individual which relates to the provision of health care should that individual become incapacitated, such as a living will or durable power of attorney for health care.

The advance directives information which the health care provider is required to provide the patient must include:

1. A description of the individual's right under state law, whether statutory or judge-made, to make decisions concerning medical care, including the right to accept or refuse treatment, and the right to formalize advance directives.
2. A description of the health care provider's written policies concerning the implementation of the patient's rights.

The PSDA also pinpoints the time at which the patient is to receive the advance directives information, depending on the type of institution, as follows:

1. A hospital is required to provide the patient with this information at the time he or she is admitted as an inpatient.

2. A skilled nursing facility is required to provide the patient with this information at the time he or she is admitted as a resident.

3. Home health agencies are required to provide the patient with this information prior to the time the individual comes under the care of the agency.

4. Hospice programs are required to provide the patient with this information at the time hospice care is initiated.

5. Health maintenance organizations are required to provide the patient with this information at the time he or she enrolls in the plan.

In addition, the advance directives information must be provided to the patient each time he or she is admitted and/or comes under the care of the particular facility. Further, if an individual is first admitted to a hospital and then later transferred to a nursing home, both the hospital and the nursing home are required to independently provide the advance directives information to the individual upon admission.

State Involvement

The PSDA requires each individual state to develop a written description of its law, whether statutory or judge-made, concerning the advanced directives that would be distributed by health care providers.

The Secretary of Health and Human Services

The PSDA requires the Secretary of the Department of Health and Human Services to:

1. Develop and implement a national campaign to inform the public of the option to execute advance directives, and of a patient's right to participate in, and control, his or her own health care decisions; and

2. Develop or approve nationwide information materials, to be distributed by health care providers, which would:

(a) inform the public and the medical and legal profession of the individual's right to make decisions concerning their medical care, including the right to accept or refuse treatment; and

(b) inform the public and the medical and legal profession of the existence of advance directives.

In addition, the Secretary is required to work with the individual states in preparing material concerning applicable state laws on the subject, to mail such information to all recipients of social security, and to include information concerning the PSDA in the Medicare handbook.

THE PATIENT'S RIGHT TO PAIN MANAGEMENT

People who experience pain have the right to receive treatment to alleviate their pain. Proper treatment of pain depends on the type, location and duration of the pain. Efforts to reduce or eliminate the pain may include evaluation and treatment by surgeons or other doctors who specialize in treating the part of the body that is believed to be the source of the pain. In general, there are three classifications of pain:

1. Acute Pain - Acute pain is usually severe and lasts for short periods of time. It can come from an accident, the onset of illness or disease, or as a result of surgery. Usually, the pain indicates that the body's tissue has been injured. Acute pain usually disappears as healing occurs.

2. Chronic Pain - Chronic pain stays for a long period of time. Chronic pain often accompanies certain diseases and conditions such as arthritis, migraine headaches, cancer, or sensitivity from an old injury or surgery.

3. Intractable Pain - Intractable pain occurs because the cause of the pain cannot be removed or otherwise treated. Intractable pain remains even after reasonable efforts have been made to reduce or eliminate it.

In order to properly understand the patient's condition and treat their pain, the health care provider should:

1. Perform a physical exam and take a history of the patient's condition.

2. Conduct any tests needed to determine the source of the pain.

3. Coordinate the patient's care with any other health care providers who are treating the patient.

4. Refer the patient to a specialist who has experience treating people with pain.

People experiencing pain have the right to be advised as to:

1. The complete and current information about their condition;

2. The range of appropriate treatment options; and

3. The prognosis for their condition.

In addition, people experiencing pain are entitled to participate fully in the decisions affecting their care, and give truly informed consent to the treatment plan their doctor recommends. Regardless of the recommended treatment, the health care provider is also required to advise the patient of the risks and benefits of all available treatments, and the goals of treatment.

People in pain have the right to receive treatment for their pain. Pain treatment may involve the use of drug and non-drug therapies, often in combination. These may include:

1. Temporary relief, such as ibuprofen and aspirin and other "over-the-counter" medications for mild to moderate acute pain.

2. Prescription pain relievers, such as anti-inflammatory drugs or opiates to manage moderate to severe pain.

3. Physical therapy or lifestyle changes.

In addition, patients have the right to choose alternative treatments to manage their pain, including physical therapy, acupuncture, biofeedback/relaxation techniques, massage, chiropractic care, psychotherapy to help manage depression that may accompany chronic or intractable pain, hypnosis, and behavior modification.

Narcotic Treatment

After evaluating the patient's condition, the health care provider may prescribe stronger medication, such as anti-depressants, nerve block injections, or opiates. Opiates, also known as narcotics, include morphine, codeine, and percodan. If the doctor will not prescribe opiates, the patient has the right to be referred to a doctor who will prescribe this pain.

Medical Marijuana

There has been much controversy about the legalization of smoked marijuana for medical purposes. One marijuana-based product, Marinol, which is the synthetic oral form of the major active ingredient in marijuana, has been approved since 1985 for the treatment of nausea and vomiting associated with cancer chemotherapy, and the FDA subsequently approved its use in loss of appetite and weight loss problems related to AIDS.

Since 1986, Marinol had been classified by the Drug Enforcement Agency (DEA) as a Schedule II drug, which placed certain restrictions on prescribing the drug. In July 1999, in accord with the scientific and medical evaluation and recommendations of HHS, the DEA lowered Marinol to a Schedule III drug. This reclassification makes the drug more available to patients, and allows physicians to write prescriptions providing as many as five refills within six months.

Approval of marijuana for medical purposes requires the same level of scientific evidence required for all other pharmaceutical products. The National Institutes of Health (NIH), a department of the Department of Health and Human Services (HHS), and the Institute of Medicine (IOM) have both conducted reviews of existing research on the possible medical effectiveness of smoked marijuana. Although both reviews have concluded that research obtained thus far has not demonstrated a therapeutic benefit, the reviews also concluded that further research was justified, especially for certain diseases.

Although the IOM study found that some chemical components of marijuana show promise for therapeutic use, it is the delivery system—i.e., smoking—that presents health risks, thus, they have called for a study of alternative delivery methods of the beneficial components of marijuana.

In order to carry out additional scientific research, HHS has created a special process that enables them to provide research grade marijuana for non-NIH funded projects found to have scientific merit, after they have obtained permission from the Drug Enforcement Agency (DEA) and an Investigational New Drug (IND) license from the Food and Drug Administration (FDA).

ASSISTED SUICIDE

Assisted suicide refers to the ending of one's life with the help of another, usually a physician. Unlike advance directives, which are passive in nature, assisted suicide actively hastens death. Assisted suicide has also been referred to as mercy killing or active euthanasia. Although society at one time shunned the concept of assisted suicide and likened it to murder, the development of the law in this area seems to show that assisted suicide is gaining acceptance.

Euthanasia, translated literally, simply means a "good death." The term has traditionally been used to refer to the hastening of a suffering person's death or "mercy killing," and it may be voluntary or involuntary. Involuntary active euthanasia is one of the least accepted social policies. It refers to an intervention that ends a patient's life without obtaining the informed consent of the patient.

Voluntary active euthanasia involves an intervention requested by a competent individual that is administered to cause death, such as a lethal injection. Although no law currently authorizes this practice, polls show that a growing number of Americans support honoring a patient's request for voluntary active euthanasia. Assisted suicide has been the subject of intense national debate.

In June, 1997 the U.S. Supreme Court handed down decisions in two cases challenging the legality of state bans on assisted suicide. In both cases the Court found that there was no constitutional right to assisted suicide and turned the matter back to states to decide whether to ban or legalize assisted suicide.

Oregon became the first state to permit physician-assisted suicide in limited circumstances when it enacted the Oregon Death With Dignity Act in 1994. Following passage of the Act, the Oregon Catholic Conference attempted to have it repealed. When that failed, they succeeded in bringing it up for a second vote which was held on November 4, 1997. The Act again passed with a resounding 60 - 40 victory, demonstrating the overwhelming support of the people for this right.

Proponents of assisted suicide see the request for assistance in dying as an extension of an individual's right to control over their end-of-life health care decisions. Opponents to the procedure fear that the "right-to-die" may eventually turn into a coercive "duty-to-die" targeted at the elderly or infirm.

A directory of national organizations supporting choice-in-dying is set forth at Appendix 10.

CHAPTER 3:
HOSPITALS AND NURSING HOMES

IN GENERAL

Hospital and nursing home patients have certain rights and protections guaranteed under federal and state laws to help ensure the quality and safety of a patient's hospital care. In addition, medical facilities are generally prohibited from discriminating against patients in the delivery of health care services based on race, ethnicity, national origin, religion, sex, age, mental or physical disability, sexual orientation, genetic information, or source of payment.

Insofar as this almanac provides a general discussion of law, the reader is advised to check their state and local law for specific rules and regulations applicable to their jurisdiction.

THE HOSPITAL'S DUTY TO ADMIT OR TREAT

Under the common law, an individual is not generally obligated to prevent an injury to another absent special circumstances. This common law doctrine includes the right of a hospital to refuse to admit or treat a person who comes in seeking admission or treatment.

The Courts have generally deferred to the medical judgment of hospital personnel, and refused to require hospitals to use their medical resources for every person seeking treatment. Nevertheless, as further discussed below, there are circumstances under which the Courts have held that the common law doctrine of "no duty to admit or treat" does not apply.

Emergency Situations

Hospitals are generally required to treat seriously injured or sick persons on an emergency basis, and their refusal to treat such people has resulted in the imposition of liability. However, the nature of an emergency is subjective and it is not always apparent whether a patient's condition actually constitutes an emergency.

In general, emergencies involve events which are sudden or unforeseen. However, even where an individual's condition is not in an emergency status at the time they arrive at the hospital, requiring that person to seek medical attention elsewhere may turn a non-emergency situation into an emergency. Thus, a hospital may also be required to prevent the occurrence of an emergency.

For example, if a woman is pregnant and in the early stages of labor, her status would not be considered an emergency. However, if requiring the woman to seek alternative medical treatment would mean that she would have to travel a very long distance, the receiving hospital may be required to treat the woman regardless of her present status.

Discrimination

Many federal and state statutes prohibit unreasonable discrimination by hospitals in their refusal to admit or treat, despite the common law doctrine.

Discrimination on the Bases of Race, Color, Religion or National Origin

Hospitals are constitutionally prohibited from refusing to treat or admit a particular person due to their race, color, religion or national origin.

Discrimination on the Basis of Inability to Pay

Hospitals are not permitted to discriminate against patients based on their inability to pay for their treatment, particularly where the hospital receives federal assistance. Under the Hill-Burton Act, 42 U.S.C. §291-2910, which established funding for construction and modernization of hospitals, a 20-year obligation was placed upon hospitals which received federal funds to provide free care and community service to indigent patients. In addition, many states have enacted legislation prohibiting hospitals from discriminating against individuals based on their ability to pay.

The Emergency Treatment and Active Labor Act (EMTALA)

Under the Emergency Treatment and Active Labor Act of 1986 (EMTALA)—also known as the "Anti-Dumping Act", medicare provider hospitals are prohibited from transferring, discharging or refusing to treat a patient solely because of his or her inability to pay for treatment where the hospital has the resources to provide the needed care. Hospitals which violate EMTALA are subject to civil liabilities, including monetary sanctions.

Under EMTALA, the hospital must provide an appropriate medical screening examination to any person seeking treatment or admission at an emergency department, to determine whether an emergency exists. If the individual refuses to submit to the medical examination, the hospital will have been deemed to have complied with the Act provided it adequately informs the individual of the risks associated with his or her refusal to be examined.

As defined by the Act, an emergency exists if the individual's medical condition could reasonably be expected to put the individual's health in serious jeopardy, or result in a serious impairment to bodily functions, or serious dysfunction of any bodily organ or part.

If the medical screening examination determines that the individual has an emergency medical condition, they may not be transferred or discharged unless their medical condition is stabilized.

The Act also applies to pregnant women having contractions if there is not enough time to safely transfer the woman to another hospital before delivery, without posing a threat to her health or safety, or the health and safety of her unborn child.

An exception to the rule exists if the patient requests a transfer, in writing, after being thoroughly advised of the risks of the transfer and the hospital's obligation to treat the patient. In addition, another exception exists if a physician certifies that the medical benefits of the transfer outweigh the risks.

Child Abuse and Rape

Federal and state regulations generally require hospitals to treat children who have been abused or raped. In addition, hospitals are also required to notify state child protective agencies when there is suspicion of child abuse under mandatory reporting statutes. Most jurisdictions grant a hospital with criminal and civil immunity from lawsuits brought as a result of reporting abuse, provided the hospital makes the report in good faith. Therefore, it is incumbent upon the hospital to make a detailed record concerning its reasons for making a report. Inadequate notes may cancel the immunity and subject the hospital to liability.

Patient Abandonment

The intentional tort of abandonment may arise in the context of the health care provider/patient relationship. For example, once a health provider undertakes to treat a patient, he or she cannot unilaterally terminate the relationship. The only circumstances under which the health care provider/patient contract can be terminated are: (1) if the patient terminates the relationship; (2) if there is termination by mutual agreement; (3) if the health care provider becomes incapacitated; (4) if the patient's illness terminates; or (5) if the treatment sought is successful.

Therefore, if a health care provider begins treatment of a patient, the health provider would be liable for abandonment if they attempt to terminate the relationship without first obtaining the consent of the patient. If a health care provider is concerned about exposure to HIV, he or she may require the patient to be tested prior to accepting the patient into treatment.

THE HOSPITAL PATIENT'S RIGHT TO INFORMATION

Hospital patients have the right to certain information concerning the hospital so that they can make an informed decision as to whether they want to undergo treatment at the particular facility. Upon request, a prospective patient should be provided with information about the facility regarding the following:

1. The corporate form of the facility—e.g., public or private; non-profit or for-profit; ownership and management; affiliation with other corporate entities.

2. The hospital's accreditation status.

3. Whether specialty programs meet guidelines established by specialty societies or other appropriate bodies—e.g., whether a cancer treatment center has been approved by the American College of Surgeons, the Association of Community Cancer Centers, or the National Cancer Institute.

4. The volume of certain procedures performed at the facility.

5. The hospital's consumer satisfaction measures.

6. The hospital's clinical quality performance measures.

7. The hospital's service performance measures.

8. The hospital's procedures for registering a complaint and achieving resolution of that complaint.

9. The availability of translation or interpretation services for non-English speakers and people with communication disabilities.

10. The numbers and credentials of providers of direct patient care—e.g., registered nurses, other licensed providers, and other caregivers.

11. Whether the hospital's affiliation with a provider network would make it more likely that a consumer would be referred to health professionals or other organizations in that network.

12. Whether the hospital has been excluded from any Federal health programs—e.g., Medicare or Medicaid.

THE PATIENT'S RIGHT TO PARTICIPATE IN HEALTH CARE DECISIONS

The hospital patient has the right to participate in decisions about their health care and to understand what they are being told about their care and treatment. For example, the patient is entitled to a clear explanation of tests, treatments and drugs prescribed for them.

In addition, some rights and protections, such as those that govern when the patient can leave the hospital, depend on the issuance of certain written notices, and information concerning appeal procedures and contacts.

For people with special needs, such as a hearing or vision disability, or the inability to understand English, hospitals must make skilled interpreters available to patients to explain and answer questions about their rights and provide information on how they can protect those rights.

Translations and/or transcriptions of important hospital forms, instructions and information must be provided if the patient requires them for an understanding of the documents.

A patient's rights to give informed consent and refuse treatment under various circumstances is more fully discussed in Chapter 2 of this almanac.

THE MATERNITY PATIENTS' RIGHT TO INFORMATION

In general, hospitals and birth centers that "prebook" maternity patients must provide these patients, at the time of prebooking, with written information that contains brief definitions of maternity-related procedures and practices, including statistics specific to each hospital.

This information is provided in order to assist the maternity patient with a better understanding of their options, so that they can make a more informed decision about their childbirth plans. Most of the statistical information is given in percentages of all the deliveries occurring in the hospital during a given year. For example, if 20 births out of 100 are by cesarean section, the cesarean rate will be 20%.

Hospitals must also generally: (1) assure that prenatal childbirth education classes are available for all prebooked women; (2) distribute newborn screening educational literature; and (3) provide all prebooked women with a written description of available options for labor, delivery and postpartum services.

HOSPITAL DISCHARGE

A hospital patient is entitled to receive all of the care necessary to treat their illness or injury. Their discharge from the hospital should be dependent on whether or not their condition has been adequately treated and they are physically ready to leave, not on whether the hospital needs the room or the patient's insurance coverage is inadequate.

Prior to discharge, the hospital is required to provide the patient with a written discharge notice. Any questions about the discharge notice should be directed to the designated hospital representative. The patient has the right to appeal the written discharge notice or plan prior to their discharge. The notice will generally set forth the appeal procedures and provide a contact name. However, if the appeal is denied, the patient will be required to pay for their continued stay at the hospital beyond their initial date of discharge.

The patient is also entitled to receive a written discharge plan prior to leaving the hospital. The discharge plan should describe the arrangements for any future health care the patient may need after discharge. In general, the patient may not be discharged until the services required in their written discharge plan are secured, or determined by the hospital to be reasonably available. Patients may also appeal their discharge plan if they disagree with it. If so, the hospital is required to provide the patient with a statement of their additional rights.

QUALITY OF CARE ISSUES

Hospital patients who believe they have received incompetent, negligent, fraudulent, or otherwise inadequate care from a doctor or physician's assistant should file a complaint with their state physician licensing bureaus. The complaint should include all relevant facts surrounding the inadequacy of care, as well as the names of all physicians and physicians assistants involved in the patient's care.

A Directory of State Physician Licensing Bureaus is set forth at Appendix 1.

Hospital patients who believe they have received incompetent, negligent, fraudulent, or otherwise inadequate care from other licensed health care professionals, such as nurses, or who have other complaints about the care they received during their hospital stay, should file a complaint with their state licensing agency for medical facilities. Again, the complaint should include all relevant facts surrounding the inadequacy of care, as well as the names of any individual health care professionals or hospital employees involved in the patient's care.

A Directory of State Licensing Agencies for Medical Facilities is set forth at Appendix 2.

HOSPITAL BILLING ISSUES

Hospital patients are entitled to receive an itemized bill of all charges incurred at the hospital. Hospital patients are also entitled to an explanation of any charges that appear on the bill that they do not understand. Questions may be directed to the hospital's billing office or the patient's insurance carrier.

ACCESS TO HOSPITAL RECORDS

A patient is entitled to access their own hospital records. Generally, the patient must send a written authorization to the hospital's medical records department. A fee may be assessed for copying the records, however, the law generally sets a ceiling on the amount a hospital can charge the patient. If the hospital fails to provide the patient with a copy of their medical records within a reasonable period of time, a complaint may be made to the appropriate state agency.

Medical records and patient confidentiality rights are discussed more fully in Chapter 4 of this almanac.

NURSING HOMES

Unfortunately, many people have health care problems which render them disabled and dependent on others to help them with their daily activities. Unlike acute care—short-term, recuperative care provided by a hospital—long-term care is the type of care given to a person who has become disabled or who suffers from a chronic illness. In such a case, important decisions must be made about the proper setting in which such care may be given.

A nursing home generally refers to a residential facility that provides shelter and care for senior citizens and other disabled individuals who are unable to live independently. Federal law guarantees nursing home residents certain rights, applicable whether it is publicly or privately owned institution. These rights include, but are not limited to:

1. The right to be free from physical or mental harm or abuse;

2. The right to privacy; and

3. The right to choose their own physician and participate in their own health care decisions.

The State Offices of Long-Term Care Ombudsman are agencies actively involved with nursing homes in an effort to improve the conditions for nursing home patients.

A Directory of the State Offices of Long-Term Care Ombudsman is set forth at Appendix 11.

Types of Nursing Homes

In general, there are three types of nursing homes:

Personal Care Nursing Facility

A Personal Care Nursing Facility provides the senior citizen who does not need any special medical care with room and board and basic assistance with daily activities. These long-term care facilities are generally not covered by Medicare and Medicaid primarily because of the lack of significant medical care needed by the residents.

Medicaid Nursing Facility

A Medicaid Nursing Facility provides the senior citizen or disabled individual with a limited range of skilled nursing care, rehabilitation services, and other necessary health-related care. Medicare does not pay for residence in such facilities, however Medicaid may reimburse the costs of such care provided a doctor certifies that the resident is in need of this level of care. Further, the resident must meet certain financial guidelines to qualify for admission.

Medicare Skilled Nursing Facility

A Medicare Skilled Nursing Facility provides the senior citizen or disabled individual with the most highly skilled nursing care available outside of a hospital setting, including many specialized services. Medicare pays up to 150 days per calendar year for residence at such a facility, provided the resident's physician certifies that they are in need of such a high level of care.

CHAPTER 4:
MEDICAL RECORDS: ACCESS AND PRIVACY ISSUES

CONTENT OF MEDICAL RECORDS

A patient's medical records generally includes all records related to the individual's health, which are prepared by or under the supervision of a health care provider. A patient's medical records come in a number of different formats, most typically as paper documents and x-rays . However other formats, such as nuclear medicine test results, Magnetic Resonance Imaging (MRI) scans, digital mammography studies, or a doctor's dictation also exist and would be considered part of the patient's medical records. In addition, certain electronic records may be included as a patient's medical records.

Certain medical records are generally not considered part of a patient's medical record, including but not limited to mental illness treatment records, alcohol and drug dependence treatment records, developmental disability treatment records, and certain HIV test results.

THE PATIENT'S RIGHT TO ACCESS MEDICAL RECORDS

Everyone has the absolute right to obtain copies of their own medical records. There are a number of circumstances under which an individual might need those records.

For example, if they believe their treatment by a certain medical provider was below acceptable standards, and they suffered injuries as a result, they may want to obtain their medical records so that an independent medical expert can review the records in anticipation of malpractice litigation. In addition, an individual may want to obtain their records to get a second opinion before undergoing medical treatment. One may also need access to their medical records in connection with disability proceedings, insurance applications, and when changing medical providers.

In order to access one's medical records, they need to submit a written request to the health care provider in possession of the records. The health care provider may have their own authorization form for the patient to complete. In general, the authorization should contain the following information:

1. The name of the patient whose record is being disclosed;

2. The type of information being disclosed.

3. The purposes of the disclosure, e.g., a disability determination, medical/legal opinion; an insurance application, etc.

4. Authorized and notarized signature and date.

The health care provider is entitled to charge reasonable costs for providing copies of the medical records. The patient usually receives copies of the records once the costs are submitted.

CORRECTING ERRORS IN THE MEDICAL RECORD

If there are errors in one's medical records, a letter may be sent to the health care provider explaining the problem, and requesting that a correction be made to the records. The patient should also request to have the letter included in their medical record.

Errors in medical transcription may occur. However, intentional falsification or destruction of a patient's medical records is illegal. If a patient suspects their medical records have been altered, destroyed, or the records are being withheld even after a signed release has been provided, the patient is advised to contact an attorney to discuss how to proceed.

PRIVACY OF MEDICAL RECORDS

Whatsoever things I see or hear concerning the life of men, in my attendance on the sick or even apart therefrom, which ought not be noised abroad, I will keep silence thereon, counting such things to be as sacred secrets. Oath of Hippocrates, 4th Century, B.C.E.

A patient's medical records are considered highly confidential due to the personal nature of the information contained in the records. Besides information about physical health, one's medical records may include information about family relationships, sexual behavior, substance abuse, and even the private thoughts and feelings that accompany psychotherapy. Patients have the right to communicate with their health care providers in confidence and to have the confidentiality of their individually identifiable health care information protected.

MEDICAL RECORDS RELEASE FORM

In order to ensure the patient's right to confidentiality, individually identifiable medical records cannot be used without the patient's written consent, except in limited circumstances for health purposes only, including the provision of health care, payment for services, peer review, health promotion, disease management, and quality assurance.

Before a medical provider can release a patient's medical records to any third parties, the patient is required to sign a medical records release. In the case of a minor child, the parent or legal guardian of the child can authorize the release of the child's medical records. Of course, as set forth above, the patient has an absolute right to obtain a copy of his or her medical records.

There are also laws which provide extra confidentiality protection for certain types of medical records. The purpose for the extra protection is to encourage people who may suffer from certain medical conditions, for which the patient may be particularly sensitive or embarrassed, to seek medical treatment. For example, federal law protects substance abuse treatment records. In addition, a number of states require special authorization for release of mental health records and/or records relating to HIV/AIDS.

UNAUTHORIZED DISCLOSURE OF MEDICAL RECORDS

Information concerning an individual's medical condition is of interest to a number of entities for a variety of reasons, including insurance carriers, employers, health care providers, government agencies, and law enforcement. Technological advances have made accessing, disseminating and sharing an individual's medical records relatively easy and swift. However, without legal safeguards, there is the potential for virtually unlimited access to an individual's medical records without his or her knowledge or consent.

The danger in allowing the unauthorized dissemination of an individual's medical records is that certain entities may adversely use this information to the patient's detriment. For example, insurance carriers may refuse to issue life and health insurance policies to those individuals they deem as risks based on their medical history.

In addition, employers may be unwilling to employ individuals who they deem are unhealthy based on their medical records. In fact, a study by the University of Illinois found that thirty five percent (35%) of Fortune 500 companies admitted to checking medical records prior to hiring or promoting employees.

Further, law enforcement agencies may access and use an individual's medical records obtained without authorization or warrant as evidence in connection with the prosecution of a criminal matter, e.g. for identification purposes.

Unfortunately, there is presently no comprehensive national policy ensuring the privacy of an individual's medical records, although some states have enacted laws in an attempt to protect their citizens from a breach of their privacy.

THE MEDICAL INFORMATION PRIVACY AND SECURITY ACT OF 1999 (S. 573)

In an attempt to protect the medical privacy of individual citizens, Congress has introduced legislation—The Medical Information Privacy and Security Act of 1999—which would require an individual's informed consent before his or her records were disclosed to third parties, except under carefully delineated circumstances.

For example, the law would permit personally identifiable medical records to be disclosed to a public health authority without consent only where the information relates to a specific public health purpose.

In addition, recognizing the societal value of medical research, the law does not restrict the use of anonymous or de-identified medical records for such research, but does regulate medical research that uses medical records containing personally identifiable information.

Further, disclosure of protected health information in civil litigation could occur only after it has been established that the information is material to the adjudication, e.g., where a litigant has placed his or her medical condition at issue.

Finally, the proposed legislation would greatly limit law enforcement access to medical records. For example, the proposed legislation requires law enforcement officers to obtain a court order, warrant or grand jury subpoena before gaining access to medical records. In addition, the law enforcement agent who wants to view medical records would be required to demonstrate probable cause to believe that:

1. The information is relevant and material to an ongoing criminal investigation;

2. The investigative needs of the agent cannot reasonably be satisfied by de-identified health information or by any other information; and

3. The law enforcement need for the information outweighs the privacy interest of the individual to whom the information pertains.

In effect, the legislation would apply a Fourth Amendment-like standard to the acquisition of an individual's medical records maintained by third parties.

In addition, the legislation further limits the use of protected health information following disclosure. For example, where protected health information has been disclosed in one investigation, it cannot be used in any other investigation unless the subsequent investigation arises out of, or is directly related to, the investigation for which the protected health information was initially obtained.

Further, the proposed legislation requires that notice be given to the individual whose records are being sought. The individual is also given the opportunity to contest the release of this information.

Selected text from the Medical Information Privacy and Security Act of 1999 (S. 573) is set forth at Appendix 12.

MAINTAINING PRIVACY

In order to make sure that only relevant information is noted in the patient's medical records, he or she should divulge only as much information as is necessary for proper treatment of their medical condition. Otherwise, personal information may inadvertently find its way into their medical records.

Also, explicit instructions should be given to the patient's medical providers that the patient should be contacted if a third party asks for copies of their records. The patient should also request the opportunity to review the records that their medical provider intends to send out, and request amendments to correct any inaccurate information contained in the records.

CHAPTER 5: PRIVATE HEALTH INSURANCE

IN GENERAL

Private health insurance is a type of insurance employees usually obtain as a benefit of their employment. The employer is generally responsible for paying all or most of the premium payments. Although the employee is generally entitled to choose the type of plan, the employer is entitled to choose the coverage options.

Individuals who work for employers who do not offer health insurance benefits, or who are self-employed, can purchase coverage on their own at generally higher rates. Sometimes unions and professional associations offer their members group rates for health insurance.

Types of Health Care Plans

As further discussed below, there are many types of health care plans that a consumer may choose from, including the traditional indemnity plan, or a managed care plan, such as an HMO, a point-of-service plan, or a preferred provider organization. The consumers' choice of a health plan has a significant impact on their ability to make other choices about health care facilities, health professionals, and treatment options.

Even in cases where consumers do not have a choice of plans, they are required to be provided with enough information on the plan in which they are enrolled to use the available services effectively. The primary responsibility of providing consumers with health plan information falls upon the plans themselves. In the case of self-insured plans, this responsibility rests with the plan sponsor, unless it is delegated or contracted to a third-party administrator.

TRADITIONAL HEALTH INSURANCE

Traditional health insurance plans—commonly referred to as "fee-for-service" plans—are basically indemnification policies. Under a fee-for-service plan, the insured generally pays a yearly deductible up-front, after which the insurance carrier picks up all or most of the remaining medical expenses for the year.

Under the fee-for-service plan, the insured retains control over choosing their own medical providers, including specialists, without the need for obtaining referrals from a primary physician. The insurance carrier is generally not involved in determining the necessity of the medical treatment.

The disadvantages to fee-for-service plans is that they require the insured to pay more out-of-pocket costs, such as the deductible. In addition, most insurance carriers only pay up to 80% of the remaining medical expenses, leaving the insured responsible for the difference. However, most insurance carriers pay 100% of out-of-pocket expenses once the insured's medical bills reach a specified amount, which is generally quite high.

If the medical provider is one who requires immediate payment, the insured may have to pay the entire bill at the time service is rendered, and then submit it to the carrier for payment of the covered amount.

In addition, insurance carriers generally refer to a chart of "reasonable and customary" medical costs, which is based on the average amount charged for similar services by other medical providers in the area. If the medical provider is one who does not adhere to such a chart, he or she may also seek the difference from the insured.

MANAGED CARE PLANS

The majority of private health insurance coverage available today contains some type of managed care plan. Managed care plans generally involve an agreement between an insurance carrier and a selected network of health care providers. There are significant financial incentives offered to the insured if they use the selected providers according to the type of plan and the procedure set forth under the specific plan.

The four basic types of managed health care plans include the: (i) Health Maintenance Organization (HMO); (ii) Preferred Provider Organizations (PPO); (iii) Exclusive Provider Organization (EPO); and (iii) Point-of-Service Plan (POS)

Health Maintenance Organization (HMO)

A Health Maintenance Organization is generally the least flexible type of managed care health plan. Under this plan, the insured is required to visit only those medical providers within the HMO plan. The HMO may be located in a central medical facility where all of the plan medical providers operate, or may consist of a network of individual offices.

Under an HMO plan, the insured must obtain permission from their assigned primary care physician before seeking medical care from a specialist. Further, if the insured seeks medical treatment from medical providers outside of the plan, he or she must generally bear the expense without reimbursement.

The advantage of an HMO plan is that the co-payment, if any, is very small, and the premiums are very low. In addition, the HMO generally offers the insured complete preventive medical care.

Preferred Provider Organization (PPO)

Under a Preferred Provider Organization plan, the insured is given a financial incentive to seek medical care from one of the medical providers in the insurer's selected network. For example, an insured typically pays a small co-payment for medical treatment by a network medical provider, e.g. 5 or 10 dollars.

If an insured elects to obtain medical care from a non-network medical provider, the procedure is similar to traditional health insurance in that the insured generally must pay the entire bill up-front and then submit the bill to the insurance carrier for reimbursement of a percentage of the medical bill, e.g., 80%. In addition, the insured may be charged a deductible for non-network medical expenses.

One advantage of a PPO is that the insured is permitted to seek medical care from a specialist without first obtaining permission from a primary physician. The specialist must be a network medical provider. However, preventive medical care may not be covered under a particular PPO plan.

Exclusive Provider Organization (EPO)

Exclusive Provider Organizations are a subset of the PPO with many of the features of the HMO. Under an EPO plan, it is even more costly to obtain medical treatment from a non-network medical provider because the insured is generally responsible for the entire cost without reimbursement.

Point of Service Plan (POS)

A Point of Service plan is similar to a PPO, however, the insured is required to obtain permission from a network primary care physician before seeking treatment from a specialist, even if the specialist is a network provider.

Nevertheless, under a POS plan, the insured still has the right to seek medical care from a non-network medical provider and be entitled to some reimbursement for the cost, although a deductible may apply. If, however, the primary care physician refers the insured to a non-network medical provider, the plan generally pays the costs.

THE CONSUMER'S RIGHT TO HEALTH PLAN INFORMATION

Consumers have the right to receive accurate, easily understood information about their health plans. Consumers joining or considering whether or not to join a health plan should receive the following information about the plan:

1. The plan's state licensure status, Federal certification, and private accreditation status.

2. The plan's consumer satisfaction measures.

3. The plan's clinical quality performance measures.

4. The plan's service performance measures—e.g., waiting time to obtain an appointment with primary care providers and specialists.

5. The plan's disenrollment rates.

6. The number of years the plan has been in existence.

7. The corporate form of the plan—i.e., whether the plan is public or private, etc.

8. Whether the plan meets state and Federal requirements for fiscal solvency.

9. Whether the plan meets state, Federal, and private accreditation standards that assure confidentiality of medical records and orderly transfer to caregivers.

10. Information on the numbers, types, board certification status, and geographic distribution of the plan's primary care providers and specialists.

11. A detailed list of names, board certification status, and geographic location of all of the plan's contracting primary care providers; whether they are accepting new patients; language(s) spoken and availability of interpreter services; and whether plan facilities are accessible to people with disabilities.

12. The plan's provider compensation methods, including base payment and additional financial incentives.

13. The rules regarding the plan's coverage of out-of-network services, and applicable rates of cost-sharing.

14. Information about circumstances under which primary care referral is required to access specialty care.

15. Information about what options exist for 24-hour coverage and whether enrollees have access to urgent care centers.

16. A detailed list of names, board certification status, and geographic location of all of the plan's contracting specialists and specialty care centers; whether they are accepting new patients; language(s) spoken and availability of interpreter services; and whether facilities are accessible to people with disabilities.

17. A detailed list of names, accreditation status, and geographic location of the plan's hospitals, home health agencies, rehabilitation and long-term care facilities; whether they are accepting new patients; language(s) spoken and availability of interpreter services; and whether they are accessible to people with disabilities.

18. Preauthorization and utilization review procedures followed by the plan.

19. The plan's use of clinical protocols, practice guidelines, and utilization review standards pertinent to a patient's clinical circumstances.

20. Whether the plan has special disease management programs or programs for persons with disabilities, and whether such programs are voluntary or mandatory.

21. Whether a specific prescription drug is included in a plan's formulary and the plan's procedures for considering requests for patient-specific waivers.

22. Qualifications of plan reviewers at the primary and appeals levels.

If the insured has asked for information that they are entitled to receive from their health plan, but they are having problems obtaining the requested information, they should put their request in writing.

A sample letter requesting information concerning health plan coverage terms is set forth at Appendix 13.

In addition, consumers who are eligible for coverage under the terms and conditions of a health plan must not be discriminated against in marketing and enrollment practices based on race, ethnicity, national origin, religion, sex, age, mental or physical disability, sexual orientation, genetic information, or source of payment.

ADEQUACY OF PROVIDER NETWORK

The National Association of Insurance Commissioners (NAIC) has developed standards for provider network adequacy that have been adopted by a number of states. When appropriately structured, a plan using a network of providers can improve the quality and coordination of care delivered to consumers through careful selection and credentialing of health care providers, and through coordination of care by primary care physicians and those with specialty training.

In general, all health plan networks should provide access to sufficient numbers and types of providers to assure that all covered services will be accessible without unreasonable delay, including access to emergency services 24 hours a day and seven days a week.

If a health plan has an insufficient number or type of providers to provide a covered benefit with the appropriate degree of specialization, the plan should ensure that the consumer obtains the benefit outside the network at no greater cost than if the benefit were obtained from participating providers.

WOMEN'S HEALTH CARE SERVICES

Morbidity and mortality associated with breast cancer, cervical cancer, ovarian cancer, and sexually transmitted diseases in women can be significantly reduced through the provision of preventive and routine gynecological services. The U.S. Preventive Services Task Force has issued recommendations pertaining to the provision of Pap smears, mammograms, and other preventive services for women.

To facilitate these objectives, women should be able to choose a qualified provider offered by a plan—such as a gynecologist, certified nurse midwife, and/or other qualified health care providers—for the provision of covered care necessary to provide routine and preventative women's health care services.

SPECIALISTS

Patients with ongoing health needs, and complex or serious medical conditions that require frequent specialty care, should have direct access to a qualified specialist of their choice within a plan's network of providers. This is especially true of those consumers who have disabling or terminal conditions.

In such cases, the traditional "gatekeeper" approach used by some health plans, whereby the patient must obtain a referral from a primary physician before receiving permission to visit a specialist, is unnecessarily inconvenient and can impede the patient's quality of care.

Under these circumstances, patients who require frequent specialty care should have direct access to their in-network specialist, and authorizations, when required, should be for an adequate number of visits under an approved treatment plan.

TRANSITIONAL CARE

Patients who are undergoing a course of treatment for a chronic or disabling condition, or pregnant women in their second or third trimester, at the time they involuntarily change health plans or at a time when a provider is terminated by a plan for other than cause, should be able to continue seeing their current specialty providers for up to 90 days, or through completion of postpartum care in the case of pregnant women, to allow for transition of care.

Providers who continue to treat such patients must accept the plan's rates as payment in full, provide all necessary information to the plan for quality assurance purposes, and promptly transfer all medical records with patient authorization during the transition period.

EMERGENCY SERVICES

Consumers have the right to access emergency health care services when and where the need arises. Determination as to whether the patient needs emergency services is made by using the "prudent layperson" standard. This standard refers to patients who visit emergency rooms with acute symptoms of sufficient severity such that a "prudent layperson" could reasonably expect the absence of medical attention to result in placing that consumer's health in serious jeopardy, serious impairment to bodily functions, or serious dysfunction of any bodily organ or part.

To ensure this right, health plans are advised to educate their members about the availability, location, and appropriate use of emergency services. Health plans using a defined network of providers should cover emergency department screening and stabilization services both in-network and out-of-network without prior authorization for use consistent with the "prudent layperson" standard.

In an emergency, it is likely that the patient may receive care at an out-of-network hospital. Most health plans require that they be notified within 24 to 48 hours when an insured receives out-of-network emergency services and/or is admitted to a hospital for emergency care. A health plan representative will probably arrange for follow-up care in another in-network facility or at the patient's home if the hospital where they received emergency care does not participate in the health plan.

PRESCRIPTION COVERAGE

A number of plans, particularly dental and mental health plans, do not have pharmacy benefits and will not cover the costs of prescription drugs. Specific information concerning pharmacy benefits may be found in the Summary Plan Description.

If the plan does have pharmacy benefits, it may require that the prescription be written by a plan doctor and filled at a participating pharmacy which has a contract with the plan. In addition, the medication may also need to be listed on the plan's "formulary," —the list of prescription drugs that are covered by the plan.

In some cases, a patient may be able to obtain coverage for a "non-formulary" drug—i.e., one that is not on the plan's formulary list. For example, if the patient is allergic to the formulary drug, or in cases where there is no formulary drug that can treat the patient's condition, the cost of the non-formulary drug should be covered. The health plan should have a procedure in place for the doctor to request coverage of a non-formulary drug for their patient. There may also be an expedited procedure in place if the requested medication is for pain management of a terminally ill patient.

A sample letter requesting coverage for a non-formulary prescription drug is attached at Appendix 14.

THE SUMMARY PLAN DESCRIPTION

Much of the above-described information may be found in the health plan's Summary Plan Description (SPD), which is required to explain the insured's health care benefits, any limits to their coverage, the health plan's policies and procedures, and the costs the insured will have to pay under the plan. The SPD is a binding agreement between the insured and the health plan. Thus, it is the insured's responsibility to familiarize themselves with the terms and provisions of the SPD.

The front of the SPD will contain a table of contents that outlines the information provided in the document. The SPD will also usually provide the insured with a list of definitions for words contained in the plan which may be unfamiliar to the reader. The SPD will also contain sections explaining how to use the plan, including:

1. The procedures for choosing a doctor or getting referrals to specialists;

2. The rules and cost of using doctors, hospitals and other providers that are not part of your health plan;

3. The rules and cost of using doctors that are part of your health plan but not part of the medical group you are assigned to;

4. The steps to follow to see a specialist, get a second opinion, or obtain emergency treatment.

The SPD also contains a section which sets forth the general provisions of the plan, including information on how the plan pays for the care provided; covered services; and procedures to follow if the insured disagrees with decisions made by the health plan.

The Benefits and Coverage section of the SPD is very important as it lists exactly which services and benefits the health plan provides to its members, including the number of visits that are covered over the course of a year. The services are generally categorized as:

1. Professional Services, including doctors and other health care providers;

2. Preventive Services, such as physical exams or certain tests;

3. Outpatient Services, such as physical therapy, mental health care or treatment at an urgent care center;

4. Hospital Services; and

5. Emergency Services.

Another important section of the SPD is the Exclusions and Limitations section, which sets forth the services and supplies that are not covered by the health plan. It also describes services that are limited under the plan. This section would also set forth how the plan handles "pre-existing conditions,"—conditions the insured received treatment for before joining the health plan. For example, there may be a waiting period before the plan will cover expenses for a pre-existing condition.

The SPD should also contain a section which sets forth the cost-sharing aspects of the plan, including copayments, deductibles, coinsurance, and maximum payments. By understanding these financial responsibilities, the insured will avoid unexpected medical costs.

FILING GRIEVANCES AND APPEALS

If a patient cannot resolve their complaint concerning their health care coverage informally, they have the right to file a formal grievance or appeal. A patient may generally challenge adverse decisions concerning denial of services, limitation on services, inadequacy of care, and billing issues, etc.

Prior to filing a formal grievance or appeal, the insured should check the provisions of their Summary Plan Description to make sure they have a basis for appeal, and for information on the plan's grievance and appeal procedures. In general, a grievance may be filed with the health plan or medical group, or both, and also with certain government or private agencies.

The patient should submit a description of their problem in writing. The written grievance should be sent by certified mail, with a return receipt requested, so that the patient can verify the date the letter was received, and the person who signed for it.

In filing a grievance or appeal, it is important to support the complaint with documentation, including but not limited to letters from the patient's health care providers; treatment guidelines demonstrating the proper treatment for the patient's condition; a copy of any disputed bills, and any other documentation relevant to the subject matter of the complaint. The patient should keep copies, or the originals, if available, of any documentation sent with the complaint.

The health plan is required to provide the patient with a written response acknowledging receipt of the complaint and setting forth their procedure for resolving the dispute. The patient is also entitled to a written decision advising them whether the relief requested in their complaint was granted or denied. Information on how to further appeal the decision should also be included with the written decision.

In some cases you may be able to appear before a committee that will hear your case. You may have to file a written request, usually within a limited amount of time from the date you received the letter from the health plan or medical group advising you of the decision. Some health plans have very specific rules concerning deadlines for filing further appeals, thus, the patient should make sure they comply with these rules so they do not forfeit their rights to appeal.

If the patient is unable to obtain any satisfaction through the health plan's internal grievance and appeal procedures, they may file their grievance with the appropriate state regulatory agency. Each regulatory agency has its own rules for when it will assist individuals with health plan grievances, thus, the reader is advised to check the law of his or her own jurisdiction in this regard.

A sample grievance letter to the state regulatory agency is set forth at Appendix 15.

Many plans use a procedure called "binding arbitration" as the final step for resolving grievances, appeals and claims. Most people sign an agreement to arbitrate disputes when they enroll in the health plan. Binding arbitration means that the decision of the arbitrator is final, and in most cases, the insured cannot thereafter take the case to civil court. If there is no binding arbitration agreement, the insured may be able to bring a civil action against the health plan, however, it is advisable to retain an attorney for further advice if this step becomes necessary.

Denial of Services and Referrals

If the patient is denied a health care service, treatment or procedure that they believe is medically necessary , and they cannot resolve the dispute informally, they should write a letter appealing the denial.

A sample appeal letter for services denied as not medically necessary is set forth at Appendix 16.

In addition, a delay or denial in providing the patient with a referral is generally made by the primary physician, with or without permission from the health plan, depending on its rules. The health plan representative can advise the patient as to who makes the final determination, and who is authorized to approve or deny the physician's referral.

If the patient believes they have an immediate need for medical services that have been delayed by the referral process, they can file an appeal with the health plan. However, if waiting for a decision on the appeal would pose a serious threat to the patient's health, such as loss of life, limb or major bodily function, they may ask for an "expedited" appeal, and the plan must respond within a very short time period—e.g., 5 days.

Coverage Denials and Limitations

If a patient is denied a health care service, treatment or procedure that the patient believes is covered by their health plan, and they cannot resolve the dispute informally, they should write a letter appealing the denial.

A sample appeal letter for services denied as not a covered benefit is set forth at Appendix 17.

Patients enrolled in an HMO or managed care plan have the right to an expedited review process if they are being asked to leave the hospital too soon following treatment, or if they feel their benefits are unfairly limited or denied, or that medically necessary services are inappropriately excluded from their coverage.

Quality of Care Issues

If the insured believes the care they have received was inadequate or improper, they should bring this matter first to the attention of the health care provider or medical facility where the care was given.

If the quality of care problem was significantly substandard, the insured should make a formal complaint with their health plan as well as the appropriate local and state medical societies, and the state medical board. Some incidents of inadequate medical care are so below the proper standard that an attorney should be contacted if significant injuries or damages resulted from the inadequate care.

For further guidance, the insured may consult their health plan's handbook, which is required to advise patients of the procedures to follow to make such complaints and obtain immediate review of inadequate health care allegations.

A sample complaint letter concerning quality of care issues is set forth at Appendix 18.

Billing Issues

If an insured receives a bill they believe the health plan should pay, they should first carefully read the bill to see if it is an actual bill and not merely an explanation of benefits paid, or other statement from the health plan. If, after examining the statement, it appears that it is a bill from a medical provider, the insured should contact their plan representative to find out whether they have received the bill and paid it.

If the insured receives an Explanation of Benefits form from their health plan that states a bill is not covered, there should be code numbers on the statement indicating why the amount was not covered. If the insured disagrees with the reason the bill is not being covered, they should contact the plan's customer service representative for an explanation, in writing, and ask that they pay the bill.

A sample letter to a health plan concerning a billing problem is set forth at Appendix 19.

If the problem is not satisfactorily resolved by the customer service representative after the informal letter request, the insured may have to file a grievance or appeal.

CHAPTER 6: THE CONSOLIDATED OMNIBUS BUDGET RECONCILIATION ACT (COBRA)

IN GENERAL

Skyrocketing medical costs have made health insurance benefits a household necessity for most Americans. Health coverage is one of the most important factors in a prospective employee's decision to accept or deny an offer of employment. Certain events, such as loss of employment, may trigger a simultaneous loss of these important benefits. In 1986, in order to try and ease the burden of health coverage termination, Congress enacted the Consolidated Omnibus Budget Reconciliation Act (COBRA).

Under COBRA, former employees and/or their families, who lose health insurance coverage due to termination of employment, divorce, death of the covered employee, or other qualifying life events, have the right to continue coverage under the employer's group health plan for limited periods of time.

COBRA generally covers group health plans maintained by employers with 20 or more employees in the prior year. Both full-time and part-time employees are counted to determine whether a plan is subject to COBRA. Each part-time employee counts as a fraction of an employee, with the fraction equal to the number of hours that the part-time employee worked divided by the hours an employee must work to be considered full-time.

COBRA applies to group health plans in private sector employment, as well as state and local government employers. A group health plan is ordinarily defined as a plan that provides medical benefits for the employer's own employees and their dependents through insurance or another mechanism such as a trust, health maintenance organization, self-funded pay-as-you-go basis, reimbursement or combination of these.

COBRA does not cover Federal government employer health plans. However, Federal employees are covered by a law similar to COBRA. Those employees should contact the personnel office serving their agency for more information on temporary extensions of health benefits.

QUALIFIED BENEFICIARIES

A qualified beneficiary is an individual covered by a group health plan on the day before a "qualifying event." The qualified beneficiary may be either a former employee, the employee's spouse, or the employee's dependent child. In certain cases, a retired employee, the retired employee's spouse, and the retired employee's dependent children may be qualified beneficiaries. In addition, any child born to, or placed for adoption with, a covered employee during the period of COBRA coverage is considered a qualified beneficiary. Agents, independent contractors, and directors who participate in the group health plan may also be qualified beneficiaries.

QUALIFYING EVENTS

Qualifying events are certain events that would cause an individual to lose health coverage. The type of qualifying event determines who the qualified beneficiaries are, and the amount of time that a plan must offer the health coverage to them under COBRA. A plan, at its discretion, may provide longer periods of continuation coverage.

Employees

The qualifying events for employees include:

1. Voluntary or involuntary termination of employment for reasons other than gross misconduct.

2. Reduction in the number of hours of employment.

Spouses

The qualifying events for spouses include:

1. Voluntary or involuntary termination of the covered employee's employment for any reason other than gross misconduct.

2. Reduction in the hours worked by the covered employee.

3. The covered employee becomes eligible for Medicare health coverage.

4. Divorce or legal separation from the covered employee.

5. Death of the covered employee.

Dependent Children

The qualifying events for dependent children are the same as those for the spouse, with the additional qualifying event of loss of "dependent child status" under the covered employee's health plan, e.g., due to age. The period of coverage depends on the qualifying event, and the status of the beneficiary seeking coverage.

NOTICE AND ELECTION PROCEDURES

The Act outlines how employees and family members may elect continuation coverage under COBRA. In addition, general rights under COBRA must be described in the summary plan description that all health plan participants receive from their employers. Plan administrators must automatically furnish the summary plan description to a participant or beneficiary within 90 days after they begin receiving benefits, or within 120 days after the plan is first subject to the reporting and disclosure provisions of the Employee Retirement Income Security Act (ERISA).

ERISA requires private-sector employers who offer group health plans to furnish modified and updated summary plan descriptions containing certain plan information as well as summaries of material changes in plan requirements.

Notice

Employers must notify plan administrators of a qualifying event within 30 days after an employee's death, termination, reduced hours of employment or entitlement to Medicare. A qualified beneficiary must notify the plan administrator of a qualifying event within 60 days after divorce or legal separation or a child's disqualification for coverage under the health plan rules.

Upon receiving notice of a qualifying event, plan administrators must notify qualified beneficiaries of their right to continue coverage under the plan, and provide a COBRA election notice. The notice must be provided in person or by first class mail within 14 days after the plan administrator receives notice that a qualifying event has occurred.

Election

Qualified beneficiaries must be given an election period during which each qualified beneficiary may choose whether to elect COBRA coverage. Qualified beneficiaries must be given at least 60 days for the election. This period is measured from the later of the coverage loss date or the date the COBRA election notice is provided. If they do not elect coverage within the 60-day period, they lose their right to continue health coverage benefits.

COBRA coverage is retroactive if elected and paid for by the qualified beneficiary. Each qualified beneficiary may independently elect COBRA coverage. However, a covered employee or the covered employee's spouse, may elect COBRA coverage on behalf of all other qualified beneficiaries. A parent or legal guardian may elect on behalf of a minor child.

Even if a qualified beneficiary waives COBRA coverage during the election period, he or she may revoke the waiver of coverage before the end of the election period. A beneficiary may then elect COBRA coverage. Then, the plan need only provide continuation coverage beginning on the date the waiver is revoked.

COVERED BENEFITS

Qualified beneficiaries must be offered the same coverage that the qualified beneficiary had immediately before qualifying for continuation coverage. Where a beneficiary had medical, hospitalization, dental, vision and prescription benefits under one or more plans maintained by the employer, he or she is entitled to continue coverage in one or all of these plans under COBRA. For example, the beneficiary can elect medical and forego dental coverage, or keep all coverage plans.

If there is a change in the benefits provided under the existing health plan maintained by the employer during the period of COBRA coverage, those changes will also apply to qualified beneficiaries under the plan.

In addition, COBRA beneficiaries remain subject to the rules of the plan and therefore must satisfy all costs related to copayments and deductibles, and are subject to catastrophic and other benefit limits.

COST OF COVERAGE

Once the employee elects COBRA coverage, they are required to pay for the coverage. However, because the former employer no longer contributes toward the premium payment, COBRA coverage is generally more expensive because those who elect COBRA coverage must pay the entire premium. Nevertheless, the premium is usually less than the premium for obtaining individual health coverage, and cannot exceed 102% of the cost to the plan for similarly situated individuals who have not incurred a qualifying event. This includes both the portion paid by the employee, and any portion paid by the employer, before the qualifying event, plus 2% for administrative costs.

COBRA premiums may be increased if the costs to the plan increase but generally must be fixed in advance of each 12-month premium cycle. The plan must allow the beneficiary to pay premiums on a monthly basis if they ask to do so, and the plan may allow the beneficiary to make payments at other intervals—e.g., weekly or quarterly.

The initial premium payment must be made within 45 days after the date of the COBRA election by the qualified beneficiary. Payment generally must cover the period of coverage from the date of COBRA election retroactive to the date of the loss of coverage due to the qualifying event.

Premiums for successive periods of coverage are due on the date stated in the plan with a minimum 30-day grace period for payments. Payment is considered to be made on the date it is sent to the plan. If premiums are not paid by the first day of the period of coverage, the plan has the option to cancel coverage until payment is received, and then reinstate the coverage retroactively to the beginning of the period of coverage.

If the amount of the payment made to the plan is made in error but is not significantly less than the amount due, the plan is required to notify the beneficiary of the deficiency and grant a reasonable period to pay the difference. The plan is not obligated to send monthly premium notices.

FILING CLAIMS

Beneficiaries submit claims to the plan in the same way they did prior to the qualifying event. Written procedures for filing claims must be contained in the summary plan description provided to the employee after their initial coverage began.

DURATION OF COVERAGE

Under COBRA, there are required minimum periods of coverage for continuation of health benefits. However, a plan may provide for longer periods of coverage beyond those required by COBRA. COBRA beneficiaries are generally eligible for group coverage during a maximum of 18 months for qualifying events due to employment termination or reduction of hours of work. Certain qualifying events, or a second qualifying event during the initial period of coverage, may permit a beneficiary to receive a maximum of 36 months of coverage.

Coverage begins on the date that coverage would otherwise have been lost by reason of a qualifying event and will end at the end of the maximum period.

CANCELLATION OF COBRA BENEFITS

Health coverage under COBRA may be canceled under the following circumstances:

1. Coverage may be terminated if the premiums are not paid on a timely basis.

2. Coverage may be terminated if the employer ceases to maintain any group health plan.

3. Coverage may be terminated if, after the COBRA election, coverage is obtained with another employer group health plan that does not contain any exclusion or limitation with respect to any pre-existing condition of the beneficiary. Nevertheless, if other group health coverage is obtained prior to the COBRA election, COBRA coverage may not be discontinued, even if the other coverage continues after the COBRA election.

4. Coverage may be terminated if, after the COBRA election, a beneficiary becomes entitled to Medicare benefits. However, if Medicare is obtained prior to COBRA election, COBRA coverage may not be discontinued, even if the other coverage continues after the COBRA election.

EXTENSION OF COVERAGE

There are special rules for disabled individuals and certain family members that may extend the maximum periods of COBRA coverage. If a qualified beneficiary is determined under Title II or Title XVI of the Social Security Act to have been disabled within the first 60 days of COBRA coverage, then that qualified beneficiary, and all of the qualified beneficiaries in his or her family, may be able to extend COBRA continuation coverage for up to an additional 11 months.

Nevertheless, qualified beneficiaries should be aware that they may lose all rights to the additional 11 months of coverage if notice of the determination is not provided within 60 days of the date of the determination and before the expiration of the 18-month COBRA continuation period. The qualified beneficiary who is disabled, or any qualified beneficiaries in his or her family, may notify the plan administrator of the determination.

For qualified beneficiaries receiving the 11 month disability extension of coverage, the premium for those additional months may be increased to 150% of the plan's total cost of coverage.

CONVERSION TO INDIVIDUAL POLICY

Some health plans allow participants and beneficiaries to convert group health coverage to an individual policy. If this option is available from the plan, you have the right to exercise the option under COBRA when you reach the end of your COBRA continuation coverage. The option must be given to enroll in a conversion health plan within 180 days before COBRA coverage ends.

The premium for a conversion policy may be more expensive than the premium of a group plan, and the conversion policy may provide a lower level of coverage. The conversion option, however, is not available if the beneficiary ends COBRA coverage before reaching the end of the maximum period of COBRA coverage.

GOVERNING LAW

The COBRA continuation coverage laws are administered by several agencies.

Private-Sector Health Plans

The Departments of Labor and Treasury have jurisdiction over private-sector health group health plans.

Information concerning disclosure or notification rights under a private-sector plan may be obtained by contacting the U.S. Department of Labor, Pension and Welfare Benefits Administration as follows:

U.S. Department of Labor
Pension and Welfare Benefits Administration
Division of Technical Assistance and Inquiries
Room N-5619
200 Constitution Ave., N.W.
Washington, D.C. 20210
Telephone: 1-800-998-7542

In addition, the Internal Revenue Service, Department of the Treasury, has issued regulations on COBRA provisions relating to eligibility, coverage and premiums in 26 CFR Part 54, "Continuation Coverage Requirements Applicable to Group Health Plans." Both the Departments of Labor and Treasury share jurisdiction for enforcement of these provisions.

Public-Sector Health Plans

The Department of Health and Human Services (HHS) administers the continuation coverage law as it affects public-sector health plans and has published Title XXII of the Public Health Service Act entitled "Requirements for Certain Group Health Plans for Certain State and Local Employees."

Information about COBRA provisions for public-sector employees may be obtained by contacting the U.S. Department of Health and Human Services as follows:

U.S. Department of Health and Human Services
Division of Cost Allocations (COBRA)
330 Independence Ave., S.W.
Room 1067, Cohen Building
Washington, D.C. 20201

CHAPTER 7: GOVERNMENT-ADMINISTERED HEALTH INSURANCE PROGRAMS

MEDICARE

Medicare is a federal health insurance program administered by the Social Security Administration (SSA), designated for seniors and people with disabilities, regardless of income. Medicare was passed into law on July 30, 1965 but beneficiaries were first able to sign-up for the program on July 1, 1966. Medicare is an entitlement program funded by payroll taxes. The Medicare program is administered by private health insurance companies who contract with the federal government to process claims.

The Medicare Patient's Statement of Rights is set forth at Appendix 20.

Eligibility and Coverage

When a person reaches age 65, he or she usually becomes eligible for Medicare. Unfortunately, Medicare does not cover all health-related expenses, and it is wise to supplement Medicare with additional health insurance coverage.

For example, Medicare does not pay for dentures and routine dental care, eyeglasses, hearing aids, prescription drugs, routine physical checkups, orthopedic devices, and non-skilled nursing home care—items that account for a considerable portion of medical expenses, particularly for senior citizens.

As set forth below, there are two parts to the Medicare policy: (i) Part A Hospitalization Coverage; and (ii) Part B Medical Coverage.

Part A Hospitalization Coverage

Part A is hospital insurance that covers hospital care as well as skilled nursing facility, hospice and home health care. Under Part A, there is a designated deductible—i.e., an initial amount one must pay for their hospitalization before Medicare begins to pay any additional expenses. This amount—known as the hospital deductible—increases every January 1st.

Medicare Part A benefits are free to most people 65 and older. In general, anyone eligible for Social Security or Railroad Retirement Benefits are also eligible for free Part A benefits. Persons who have been receiving Social Security disability benefits for a period of 24 months also qualify for Part A hospital coverage. Others may be eligible for Medicare if they pay a monthly premium.

If an individual has enrolled in Medicare and is also working and covered under their employer's group health plan, Medicare is still the primary payer if the employer has less than 20 employees. Medicare is the secondary payer if the employer has 20 or more employees and provides group health insurance. However, because Medicare Part A is free, an eligible individual should sign up for Part A once they are eligible, whether or not they have other insurance.

Eligible persons receive a health insurance card, known as a Medicare card, to claim their benefits. Persons already receiving Social Security automatically receive Medicare cards as part of their Social Security benefits.

Under Part A, the duration of care per benefit period is limited. A *benefit period* begins when the patient first enters a hospital or other facility, and ends after he or she has been discharged from the facility for a continuous period of at least 60 days from the date of discharge. This rule is simply a measurement device. There is no limit to the number of periods in which one may receive benefits. The benefit periods depend on the type of care received, as follows:

Hospital Care

Part A entitles the patient to 90 days of in-hospital care for each *benefit period*. There is a deductible for each benefit period. In addition, the patient has to pay a *co-insurance amount* for days 61 through 90. After the patient has exhausted their 90 days of coverage, Medicare will pay for an additional 60 days of care during the patient's lifetime. The patient will have to pay a portion during these "reserve" days. Additional coverage may be obtained through the purchase of a MediGap policy, which is further discussed below.

Hospitals cannot refuse patients on the ground that their health coverage is through Part A of Medicare. Remember, though, not all hospital stays or services are covered by Medicare. It is the hospital's responsibility to inform you if something is not covered.

Skilled Nursing Facility Benefits

Part A entitles the patient to 100 days of care in a Medicare-certified skilled nursing facility (SNF) per benefit period, provided: (i) the patient was hospitalized for at least three days during the 30 days prior to admission in the SNF and (ii) the patient needs and receives daily skilled services. Medicare defines "daily" as seven days a week of skilled nursing and five days a week of skilled therapy. Skilled nursing and therapy services include evaluation and management as well as observation and assessment of a patient's condition. Medicare pays for the first 20 days in full. For days 21 through 100, the patient pays a portion of the costs.

Home Health Care Benefits

Medicare Part A covers up to 35 hours a week of home health aide and *skilled nursing services* if a patient is homebound and requires skilled services on an *intermittent* basis. *Skilled nursing services* include the administration of medication, tube feedings, catheter changes and wound care. *Intermittent* usually means less than five days per week, but some people who receive home health care services up to seven days a week will be covered if the services are only needed for a finite and predictable amount of time. A patient can also qualify for up to 35 hours per week of home health aide services if they are homebound and need skilled physical, speech or occupational therapy.

To be covered, the patient must receive services from a Medicare-certified Home Health Agency (CHHA). Medicare home health coverage is available indefinitely so long as the patient remains homebound and continues to require skilled nursing services on an intermittent basis or skilled therapy services.

There is no prior hospitalization requirement and the benefit covers individuals with chronic illnesses as well as those who are acutely ill. The benefit is available at no cost to the patient, and there is no deductible or co-insurance required.

Hospice Benefits

Under Part A, hospice benefits are available to terminally ill patients. Medicare will cover 95 percent of the cost of hospice care, and the patient will have to pay the remaining five percent. Once the patient elects Medicare hospice benefits, he or she becomes ineligible to receive benefits for hospital care related to the terminal illness.

Part B Medical Coverage

Part B of the medicare policy covers most reasonable and necessary health-related expenses, other than hospitalization, including certain physician services, therapy services, outpatient hospital care, laboratory and diagnostic tests, supplies, durable medical equipment such as a wheelchair, and many other specified medical expenses not covered by Part A. Medicare sets approved charges for all of the medical services it covers.

Medicare does not cover many common health expenses, such as prescription drugs, routine checkups, vision and hearing care, custodial care, or dental care. It also does not cover experimental procedures.

In 1997, Congress passed a law which set forth new covered preventive care services at no extra cost, including: (i) yearly mammograms; (ii) pap smears including pelvic and breast examinations; (iii) colorectal cancer screening; (iv) bone mass measurement; (v) flu and pneumococcal pneumonia shots; and (vi) diabetes glucose monitoring and diabetes education for individuals with diabetes.

Anyone who is eligible for Part A hospital coverage is eligible for Part B medical coverage, however, Part B is not free. There is a monthly premium that increases every January 1st.

Part B medical coverage, unlike Part A, is based on a calendar year, rather than on benefit periods. The Part B medical coverage yearly deductible is $100.00 dollars. After the deductible is paid, Medicare pays 80% percent of the approved reasonable charges for covered services for the balance of the year.

Unfortunately, many health care providers charge substantially more than Medicare's approved charge for their services, and the patient must pay for any charges that are above the approved Medicare rate. For example, there is no limit on what ambulance companies and durable medical equipment suppliers may charge. The Medicare-approved portion may represent only a small part of the total bill.

Some health care providers, however, "take assignment," which means that they agree to accept Medicare's approved charge as payment in full. Medicare pays 80% of the approved charge, and the patient pays the remaining twenty percent. The local Medicare carrier has a directory that lists all doctors and suppliers in a particular area who always take assignment. To limit the amount one pays for medical expenses, it is a good idea to obtain a copy of this directory and use it when choosing health care providers.

When doctors don't "take assignment," federal law limits the amount that they may charge Medicare patients to 15% above Medicare's approved charge. Some states, including Massachusetts, Minnesota, Rhode Island, Pennsylvania, Ohio, Connecticut, Vermont and New York, have even stricter limits.

If an individual waits to enroll in Part B until he or she is older than 65, their monthly premium may be higher, since Medicare imposes a ten percent premium penalty for every year enrollment is delayed. However, if an individual is working and covered under their employer's group health plan, they may delay enrolling without a penalty until seven months after retirement.

However, it may not be cost-effective to sign up for Part B if you are already covered under an employer group health plan. That's because you will have to pay Medicare's Part B monthly premium and annual deductible, and your returns will be limited. In addition, it may be wise to stay in your employer's health plan after retirement, if that is an option, since any new insurance plans, including Medigap, may exclude pre-existing health problems for up to six months.

Medicare + Choice

In 1997, Congress passed a law which made many changes in the Medicare program, including a new provision known as *Medicare + Choice*, which creates new health plan options for Medicare recipients.

Under the new law, a Medicare recipient can decide to: (i) continue receiving Medicare benefits under the original Medicare plan, (ii) continue receiving Medicare benefits under the original Medicare plan supplemented by one of ten available Medigap insurance policies, as further discussed below; or (iii) change to a plan that gives them at least the same, and possibly more, benefits than under the original Medicare plan.

There are differences among the new health plans including: (i) the cost; (ii) the availability of extra benefits; and (iii) the participant's choice in using certain doctors, hospitals and other medical providers.

In order to be eligible for Medicare + Choice, a recipient must have Medicare Parts A and B, and not have permanent kidney failure. Nevertheless, no matter which health plan option one chooses, they are still in the Medicare program and are still entitled to all of the services Medicare covers.

Additional health care options available under the Medicare + Choice program include:

Medicare Managed Care Plan

A Medicare managed care plan is a Medicare approved network of doctors, hospitals, and other health care providers that agrees to give care in return for a set monthly payment from Medicare. Some managed care plans may provide extra benefits, and some may charge the participant a premium.

A managed care plan may be any of the following: (i) A Health Maintenance Organization (HMO); (ii) Provider Sponsored Organization (PSO); Preferred Provider Organization (PPO); or a Health Maintenance Organization with a Point of Service Option (POS).

An HMO or PSO usually asks the participant to use only the doctors and hospitals in the plan's network. If so, there are little or no out-of-pocket cost for covered services. A PPO or POS usually lets the participant use doctors and hospitals outside of the plan for an extra out-of-pocket cost.

A private fee-for-service plan (PFFS) is a Medicare approved private insurance plan. Medicare pays the plan a premium for Medicare-covered services. A PFFS Plan provides all Medicare benefits. A PFFS Plan is not the same as a Medigap policy.

The PFFS Plan, rather than Medicare, decides how much to pay for the covered services the participant receives. Providers may bill the participant more than the plan pays, up to a limit, and the participant must pay the difference. It is likely that the participant will pay a premium for a PFFS plan.

A Medicare medical savings account plan (MSA) is a health insurance policy with a high yearly deductible. This is a test program for up to 390,000 Medicare beneficiaries. Medicare pays the premium for the Medicare MSA Plan and deposits money into a separate Medicare MSA established by the participant. The participant uses the money in the Medicare MSA to pay for medical expenses.

The participant can accumulate money in their Medicare MSA to pay for extra medical costs. The insurance policy has a high deductible and there are no limits on what providers can charge above what is paid by the Medicare MSA Plan. A participant can only enroll in a Medicare MSA Plan during the month of November, and must remain in the plan for a full year.

Further information about the Medicare + Choice program may be obtained from the State Health Insurance Assistance Program in an individual's area. The State Health Insurance Assistance Program will help an individual with Medicare questions or provide information about other available health care options.

Senior citizens wishing to contact their government representatives in connection with health initiatives of interest to the elder population can contact the Congressional Committees on Aging at the following addresses:

The House of Representatives:
House Select Committee on Aging
712 House Office Building, Annex #1
Washington, DC 20515-6361
Tel: 202-226-3375

The Senate:
Senate Special Committee on Aging
Dirksen Senate Office Building, Room SD-G41
Washington, DC 20510-6400
Tel: 202-224-5364

Denial of Claims Under Medicare Part A Hospital Coverage

Under Medicare Part A hospital coverage, if a Medicare claim is denied, the hospital or Medicare review board must inform the claimant in writing if their stay will not—or will no longer—be covered by Medicare. The denial notice will set forth the procedures to follow in order to have the denial reconsidered. Many such denials are overturned.

If, after reconsideration, the claimant is still not satisfied, there are further remedies for appealing the decision. A large number of appeals are successful.

Hospital Discharge

Medicare patients have the same rights as all other patients to remain in the hospital until their medical condition dictates that they are ready to be discharged. According to federal law, the Medicare patient's discharge date must be determined solely by their medical needs, not by Medicare payments.

If a Medicare patient believes they are being asked to leave the hospital too soon, and have not received advance notice telling them when to leave the hospital, the patient should ask for their discharge notice—also called a Hospital Issued Notice of Noncoverage (HINN). In order to appeal the discharge decision, the patient needs this written discharge notice.

The Medicare patient has the right to request a review by a Peer Review Organization (PRO) of the written Notice of Noncoverage that they receive from the hospital, stating that Medicare will no longer pay for their hospital stay. Peer Review Organizations are groups of doctors who are paid by the federal government to review medical necessity, appropriateness and quality of hospital treatment furnished to Medicare patients.

If the hospital and the patient's doctor agree with the hospital's discharge decision, Medicare will no longer pay for the patient's hospital care and the patient will be issued a Notice of Noncoverage. The patient can then request the PRO to review the case. As part of their review, the PRO must ask the patient for their views about their case before making their decision. The PRO will inform the patient by phone, and in writing, of its decision on the review.

In general, if the patient requests the review by noon of the first business day after they receive the Notice of Noncoverage, the patient cannot be required to pay for any extended hospital care until the PRO makes its decision. If the PRO agrees with the Notice of Noncoverage, the patient may be billed for all costs of their stay beginning at noon of the day after they receive the PRO's decision. Thus, the patient will not be responsible for the cost of their hospital care before they receive the PRO's decision.

If the patient fails to request a review, the hospital may bill the patient for all the costs of their hospital stay beginning with the third day after the patient is given the Notice of Noncoverage. There is one exception to this rule for the few hospitals that are designated by Medicare as "non-PPS hospitals." Medicare patients in such hospitals may be billed for all costs of their extended stay beginning the day following the day of the patient receives the Notice of Noncoverage.

Nevertheless, if the hospital fails to provide the patient with a Notice of Noncoverage, then the hospital cannot charge the patient for the extended care.

If the hospital and doctor disagree with the hospital's decision to discharge the patient, the hospital may request the PRO to review the case. If it does make such a request, the hospital is required to send the patient a notice to that effect. In this situation, the PRO must agree with the hospital or the hospital cannot issue a Notice of Noncoverage.

Billing Issues

Hospital patients are entitled to an adequate explanation of the costs which appear on the hospital bill. Medicare patients who have questions about their hospital bill may call: 1-800-331-7767.

Denial of Claims Under Medicare Part B Coverage

Under Medicare Part B coverage, if a claim is denied, the claimant will receive an "Explanation of Medicare Benefits." The claimant then has six months to ask for the denial to be reconsidered and overturned. If the claim is again rejected, the claimant has an additional six months to request a hearing through their local Medicare carrier. If the claim is again denied, the claimant has 60 days to request a hearing before an administrative law judge.

SUPPLEMENTAL HEALTH INSURANCE PROGRAMS

Medigap Insurance

Medicare does not pay for all of an individual's medical expenses. Therefore, eligible Medicare recipients may also purchase supplemental coverage known as Medigap insurance. Medigap policies generally pay for medical-related expenses not reimbursed by Medicare, such as hospital deductibles and co-payments.

Medigap policies are designed to supplement Medicare and generally do not cover long-term care, although some policies do provide for skilled nursing home care and at-home recovery care. There are ten variations of Medigap plans available through private insurance companies. The basic benefits offered under all plans include:

1. Hospital co-insurance;

2. Full coverage for 365 additional hospital days to be used after exhaustion of Medicare hospital reserve days;

3. Twenty percent co-payment for physician and other Part B services; and

4. Three pints of blood.

There are a number of additional benefits available depending upon the plan you select. These benefits include:

1. Coverage of the Medicare hospital deductible;

2. Skilled nursing facility daily co-insurance;

3. Coverage of the Part B $100 deductible;

4. Eighty percent of emergency medical costs outside the U.S. during the first two months of a trip;

5. Payment to cover the difference when a doctor's fees are over the Medicare-approved charge;

6. At-home custodial care in addition to and in conjunction with Medicare-approved home care;

7. Some prescription drug coverage; and

8. Some preventive medical care coverage.

There are many services a Medigap plan will not cover. These include:

1. Custodial care—such as feeding, bathing and grooming—either at home or in a nursing home;

2. Long-term skilled care in a nursing home;

3. Unlimited prescription drugs;

4. Vision care;

5. Dental care; or

6. Private nurses.

In addition, if Medicare refuses to cover medical care because it is unreasonable and unnecessary or experimental, Medigap will not cover it either.

Once you select a Medigap policy, you have 30 days to review the plan and cancel it without penalty. You also are allowed to change or cancel your policy once a year, although in most states your insurer can reject your application for more comprehensive coverage. However, if you wish to downgrade your policy, you may do so.

If an individual does opt to enroll in a Medigap plan, it's usually best to do so during the six months following enrollment in Medicare Part B. During that period, insurance companies must let the insured sign up for the plan of their choice, without regard to health or age.

Further information concerning Medigap insurance policies may be obtained from the National Insurance Consumer Helpline at (800) 942-4242.

MEDICAID

The Medicaid program was established in 1965 as an amendment to the Social Security Act of 1935 and was administered by the Social Security Administration until 1977. In 1977, administration of the Medicaid program was transferred to the Department of Health and Human Services and to the Health Care Financing Administration. The Medicaid program continued to be administered by the Health Care Financing Administration until June 2001, when the agency was renamed the Centers for Medicare and Medicaid Services (CMS).

Medicaid is jointly financed and administered by the federal and state governments as the primary source of health care coverage for low-income individuals, as well as the blind, and disabled populations in America. Each state has its own rules concerning eligibility and coverage, which may be complex, therefore, the reader is advised to check the law of his or her own jurisdiction for specific rules.

Eligibility

In general, to be eligible for Medicaid, a person must fit into a Medicaid eligibility category. Once a person is determined to fit into a Medicaid eligible category, the applicant's financial situation is examined. The applicant's income and resources are analyzed using a formula involving exemptions and deductions to determine the applicant's "countable" income and resources.

The applicant's countable income is then compared to the income guideline set by the state—i.e., the maximum amount of income a person can have and still be eligible for Medicaid, and their countable resources are compared to the state's resources guideline. If the applicant's income is less than or equal to the guideline, the person is considered income-eligible. A similar analysis is made of the applicant's resources. If it is determined that the applicant is both income-eligible and resource-eligible, he or she is considered qualified for Medicaid benefits.

Federal Requirements

Although states have discretion in setting their own income and resources guidelines, in order to qualify for federal funds, the federal government requires the states to provide Medicaid coverage under certain circumstances to specified groups. For example, states are required to cover:

1. Low income families with children, as described in Section 1931 of the Social Security Act, who meet certain eligibility requirements;

2. Recipients of Supplemental Security Income (SSI), which generally includes the needy elderly, the blind and disabled;

3. Infants born to Medicaid-eligible pregnant women. In such cases, Medicaid eligibility must continue throughout the first year of the

child's life provided the infant remains in the mother's household and the mother remains eligible, or would be eligible if she were still pregnant.

4. Children under age 6 and pregnant women whose family income is at or below 133 percent of the Federal poverty level. States are also required to extend Medicaid eligibility until age 19 to all children born after September 30, 1983 in families with incomes at or below the Federal poverty level.

5. Recipients of adoption assistance and foster care under Title IV-E of the Social Security Act;

6. Certain Medicare beneficiaries, as set forth below; and

7. Groups who may be eligible for Medicaid on a temporary basis, including: (i) individuals who lose SSI payments due to earnings from work or increased Social Security benefits; (ii) families who are provided 6 to 12 months of Medicaid coverage following loss of eligibility under Section 1931 due to earnings, or (iii) families who are provided 4 months of Medicaid coverage following loss of eligibility under Section 1931 due to an increase in child or spousal support.

The Medicare/Medicaid Relationship

As set forth above, the Medicare program provides hospital insurance, known as Part A coverage, to persons aged 65 and older who have insured status under Social Security or Railroad Retirement. Supplementary medical insurance, known as Part B coverage, requires payment of monthly premiums.

Medicare recipients who have low income and limited resources may receive help paying their out-of-pocket medical expenses from their state's Medicaid program. This is generally referred to as "dual eligibility." Services that are covered by both programs are paid first by Medicare, and the difference is paid Medicaid, up to the state's designated limit.

Medicaid also covers additional services, such as prescription drugs, hearing aids, eyeglasses, and nursing facility care beyond the time period covered by Medicare.

The Qualified Medicare Beneficiary Program

Persons who receive Medicare and have income and resources below a certain amount may be eligible for the Qualified Medicare Beneficiary (QMB) program. Under the QMB program, Medicaid may make certain payments on behalf of qualified Medicare recipients. For example, Qualified Medicare Beneficiaries with resources at or below twice the standard allowed under the SSI program, and income at or below 100% of the Federal poverty level, do not have to pay their monthly Medicare premiums, deductibles, and coinsurance.

Specified Low-Income Medicare Beneficiaries with resources at or below twice the standard allowed under the SSI program and income exceeding the Qualified Medicare Beneficiary level, but less than 120% of the federal poverty level, do not have to pay the monthly Medicare Part B premiums.

The Medically Needy

Although not mandatory, states may extend Medicaid eligibility to the "medically needy,"—i.e., individuals who may have too much income to qualify under the mandatory needy groups. This group is able to "spend down" to Medicaid eligibility by incurring medical and expenses to offset their excess income, thereby reducing it to a level below the maximum allowed by the state's Medicaid plan. However, states may only offer medically needy coverage to the aged, blind, and disabled populations if they also offer it to pregnant women and children.

Spending Down

To illustrate the "spending down" requirement, assume the state's medically needy income level is set at $600 per month. If the medically needy individual has a monthly income of $800 per month, he or she must "spend down" $200 per month to be eligible for Medicaid benefits. The spend down amount is multiplied by the state's budget period to determine the total spend down requirement. Once the individual's medical bills reach the total spend down requirement, he or she is then covered by the Medicaid program for the remainder of the budget period.

Poverty Level Groups

Under the Omnibus Budget Reconciliation Act of 1986, states were also given the option to extend benefits to all aged and disabled persons with incomes up to 100% of the federal poverty level. States are also free to apply less restrictive methods when determining how to count income and resources for this group.

Home Health and Nursing Home Care

Medicaid is the primary public provider for home health and nursing home care. Medicaid covered 40 percent of long-term care expenses for the elderly in 2000. Through Medicaid, states have substantial flexibility to provide home and community-based services as an alternative to institutional care. Medicaid supports approximately 260 state home and community-based service waivers that provide beneficiaries with alternatives to institutional care and enable seniors and people with disabilities to receive services at home.

The Special Income Rule

When long-term care is unavoidable, Congress gave states the option to use a special income rule to provide Medicaid to persons in institutions who have too much income to qualify for SSI benefits, but not enough income to cover their expensive long-term care. Under the special income rule, states may set a special income standard of up to 300% of the maximum SSI benefit.

The income standard applies to gross income only without exemptions or deductions. The resource standards are generally the same as those in the SSI program. In addition, the states must allow nursing facility residents to retain a small amount of their income as an allowance for personal items.

Spousal Impoverishment Provisions

Each state also has spousal impoverishment provisions which provide that when one spouse is institutionalized for at least 30 days, the other spouse, referred to as "the community spouse," does not lose all income and resources. In such a case, the community spouse's income is not considered available to the institutionalized spouse. The purpose of this rule is to protect the community spouse from becoming impoverished and in need of public assistance.

To determine the community spouse's share of resources, the couple's resources are combined and then divided in half to determine the spousal share. The spousal share is then compared to the state's community spouse protected resource amount (CSRA), and the amount actually protected for the community spouse is the greater of either the spousal share or the CSRA. The couple's home, household goods, automobile, and burial funds are not included in the calculation.

In setting a CSRA, the state may exceed the federally prescribed minimum, but may not exceed the federal maximum.

The Medicaid Recipient's Right to Appeal

The Federal Medicaid statute requires State agencies to provide beneficiaries with a fair hearing and an administrative appeal when their eligibility or requests for services are denied or not acted upon within reasonable time. These State agency determinations can be challenged in State court under State administrative procedure acts or in Federal court.

In addition, HMOs that contract to serve Medicaid beneficiaries must establish an internal complaint procedure that will resolve disputes promptly. These internal procedures are subject to review and approval by the State. Medicaid HMO enrollees have the same rights to administrative appeal as do fee-for-service enrollees.

THE STATE CHILDREN'S HEALTH INSURANCE PROGRAM (SCHIP)

The State Children's Health Insurance Program (SCHIP) is a program created under the Social Security Act that provides health insurance coverage to children whose families have incomes that are too high to qualify for Medicaid but too low to afford private health insurance. SCHIP is a partnership between the federal and state governments. Under the program, states may choose to expand their Medicaid programs, design a separate child health program, or use a combination of both.

States choosing separate child health programs must offer either the same or "equivalent" benefits as those offered under one of three benchmark plans: (i) the standard Blue Cross/Blue Shield Preferred Provider Option offered by the Federal Employees Health Benefit Program; (ii) a health benefit plan offered by the state to its employees; or (iii) the HMO benefit plan with the largest commercial enrollment in the state. If a state expands its Medicaid program, existing Medicaid limits apply.

SCHIP regulations provide certain protections to enrolled children, including access to health care specialists, access to emergency services when and where the need arises, an assurance that doctors and patients can openly discuss treatment options, and access to a fair, unbiased and timely appeals process.

CHAPTER 8: RIGHTS RELATED TO HIV/AIDS TESTING AND DISCLOSURE

HIV/AIDS TESTING

There have been many attempts to have the government initiate mandatory testing in order to stop the spread of AIDS. These attempts have been met with strong opposition. Proponents for mandatory testing claim that individuals who test positive can take precautionary measures to prevent further spread of the disease. However, opponents of mandatory testing, such as The American Civil Liberties Union (ACLU), have made a number of arguments against mandatory testing, stating that:

1. Testing does not change behavior and cannot stop the spread of the disease.

2. Testing may force people to avoid seeking health care.

3. Testing is undertaken on a mass scale thus there is a the probability that many people will either test falsely positive or falsely negative, causing unnecessary suffering and resulting in limited value.

4. Potential discoverability and abuse of the collected data would increase the vulnerability of large numbers of people to discrimination, and infringe on their constitutional right to privacy, as further discussed below.

A table of state laws concerning issues related to HIV testing is set forth in Appendix 21, and a sample informed consent to perform an HIV Test is set forth at Appendix 22.

Premarital HIV Testing

Presently, there is no state that requires HIV-testing in order to obtain a marriage license. A number of states had considered passing such legislation, however, the few that did enact and enforce premarital HIV testing subsequently repealed their laws. Nevertheless, state legislators continue to consider such legislation.

Proponents of mandatory premarital HIV-testing argue that identifying infected persons would assist in preventing HIV transmission by alerting the prospective spouse to the risk of exposure, and would further prevent the birth of HIV-infected babies. They also argue that a number of states test for other sexually transmitted diseases, such as syphilis, prior to issuing a license.

Opponents of premarital HIV-testing argue that the benefits of such a requirement are few and not cost-effective. Premarital HIV-testing is expensive and research has shown that such testing only results in identifying a negligible number of HIV-infected individuals, in large part because individuals seeking marriage licenses constitute a very low-risk population. They also argue that the money spent in operating such a program could be better spent on HIV/AIDS research and treatment and, as an alternative to mandatory testing, funding for AIDS education programs for marriage license applicants.

Mandatory Testing of Newborn Infants

The House and Senate have agreed upon a provision which requires states to conduct mandatory HIV testing of newborns. Obviously, once identified, drug therapy can be immediately employed. However, according to the CDC, because HIV antibody crosses the placenta, its presence in a child aged less than 18 months is not diagnostic of HIV infection. Therefore, a definitive determination must be made by laboratory testing.

A sample Informed Consent to Perform an Expedited HIV Test in the Delivery Setting is set forth at Appendix 23.

Mandatory Testing of Sexual Assault Defendants

Since the emergence of HIV and AIDS, society and the courts have become increasingly concerned with the possibility of HIV transmission during sexual relations and as a result of sexual assault or abuse. As further discussed below, many states have enacted criminal statutes which address these issues.

There has been much controversy over whether or not a defendant in a sexual assault case can be compelled to undergo HIV testing, particularly prior to conviction for the sexual assault. Obviously, the sexual assault victim is concerned over whether they have been exposed to the virus, and wants the defendant tested. However, opponents of involuntary testing argue that testing will not prove that the infection was transmitted to the victim, and because of the lag time between exposure and positive testing, it does not provide the victim with any reassurance that they were not exposed. Thus, the victim must still deal with the anxiety of wondering whether they were infected, and whether they are capable of infecting others.

Nevertheless, proponents of compulsory testing argue that there is some psychological benefit to the victim where the defendant tests negative, even if this does not guarantee there was no exposure. Further, if the defendant tests positive, the victim will be able to timely avail themselves to rapidly developing prophylactic treatment of HIV.

In jurisdictions which do not provide any statutory basis for compelling a defendant to undergo an HIV blood test, such a concession may be made as part of any plea bargain arrangement offered by the prosecution.

Disclosure of Test Results

There is also concern over the disclosure of the defendant's private medical record. The extent to which such records can be disclosed varies among the states. Federal law provides that disclosure of the test results can only be given to the victim, the victim's parents or guardians, and the defendant. The victim, in turn, can disclose the results to his or her medical providers, family members and any sexual partner(s) the victim may have had since the attack.

Prisoners and convicted offenders have a constitutional right of privacy that protects them from unwarranted disclosure of their HIV status even if they are subjected to mandatory testing. Thus, where a defendant has not yet been convicted of the crime, there must be adequate safeguards in place to guarantee the confidentiality of the defendant's medical records.

PARTNER NOTIFICATION STATUTES

"Partner notification" refers to the process of identifying sex and/or needlesharing partners of individuals infected with HIV or another infectious communicable disease, and advising those partners that they have been exposed to the disease. The rationale behind partner notification is that it allows identification, treatment, and education of individuals who have been exposed to a communicable disease, preventing the spread of the disease and helping people understand how to avoid future infection,

Voluntary partner notification plans encourage an infected individual to notify his or her partners and are viewed as an important component of effective HIV prevention and treatment. However, there has been much criticism of mandatory notification laws. The ACLU has strongly denounced such statutes, stating that available evidence does not justify coercive partner notification but rather demonstrates that mandatory partner notification will not work.

There is much concern that mandatory notification will deter people from getting tested in the first place. In addition, because there is no known drug therapy that will cure HIV, or prevent its transmission, and the incubation period is so long, it makes it difficult for patients to identify and locate past partners. Further, there are serious concerns about confidentiality and social stigma attached to the disease.

Nevertheless, because of the development of successful drug therapies that have allowed HIV-infected individuals to live longer and healthier lives—particularly when the treatment is started as soon as the infection has been diagnosed—there has been a movement toward mandatory partner notification.

A table of state statutes concerning partner notification is set forth at Appendix 24.

The Center for Disease Control and Prevention (CDC) has developed guidelines that urge states to formulate voluntary, confidential partner notification services. While some states have followed these guidelines, others have opted to include mandatory notification provisions. In those jurisdictions, an HIV-infected individual who fails to notify their present and past partners is subject to a fine and/or imprisonment. Some jurisdictions require the health care providers to undertaken notification regardless of whether the patient has already done so, and whether or not the patient has consented to the notification.

HIV/AIDS REPORTING REQUIREMENTS

All states require AIDS reporting and the majority of states require some reporting for HIV. However, privacy and confidentiality regulations concerning the storage, access, and uses of such information vary among jurisdictions. Thus, there is an increased need for uniformity among state confidentiality protections.

In response to this concern for a patient's right to privacy, the Centers for Disease Control and Prevention (CDC), the Council of State and Territorial Epidemiologists (CSTE), the Association of State and Territorial Health Officials (ASTHO), the National Conference of State Legislatures (NCSL), and Georgetown University Law Center (GULC) have joined together to develop, draft, and implement a model state privacy law pertaining to the use of public health information, particularly information gathered pursuant to HIV/AIDS reporting requirements.

The model privacy law is designed to protect confidential identifiable information from unauthorized publication and uses without significantly limiting the ability of health departments to use such information for legitimate public health objectives.

Selected provisions of the Model State Public Health Privacy Act are set forth at Appendix 25.

PHYSICIAN ABANDONMENT OF AIDS PATIENTS

The intentional tort of abandonment may arise in the context of the physician/patient relationship. For example, once a physician undertakes to treat a patient, he or she cannot unilaterally terminate the relationship. The only circumstances under which the physician/patient contract can be terminated are:

1. If the patient terminates the relationship;
2. If there is termination by mutual agreement;
3. If the physician becomes incapacitated;
4. If the patient's illness terminates; or
5. If the treatment sought is successful.

Therefore, if a physician begins treatment of a patient, and during the course of that treatment learns that the patient is HIV-infected, the physician would be liable for abandonment if he or she attempts to terminate the relationship without first obtaining the consent of the patient. If a physician is concerned about exposure to HIV, he or she may require the patient to be tested prior to accepting the patient into treatment.

The American Medical Association, as well as certain state licensing boards, have set forth ethical guidelines which provide that physicians who are able to treat an HIV-infected person should do so. Further, certain statutes prohibiting discrimination against the disabled—including HIV/AIDS patients—also limit the physician's right to refuse to treat such individuals. These restrictions on the right to refuse a patient have also been made applicable to private hospitals under state and federal anti-discrimination statutes.

TRANSMISSION CONCERNS IN THE HEALTH CARE SETTING

There is growing concern over both the treatment of HIV-infected patients by uninfected health care workers, and the treatment of uninfected patients by HIV-infected health care workers. A number of legal issues have arisen from these scenarios, as further discussed below.

Duty to Protect Uninfected Patients

The courts have held that health care providers, including hospitals, have a duty to protect uninfected patients from contracting HIV from other patients or infected health care providers. It is not likely that the virus would be transmitted between patients who only have casual contact with each other. It is more likely that an uninfected patient may contract HIV from the health care provider, particularly if invasive-type procedures are being performed, e.g. surgery.

Some jurisdictions require health care providers to disclose their HIV status to patients as part of the informed consent requirement. Nevertheless, a health care provider is prohibited from unnecessarily disclosing the HIV status of a patient. If so, the health care provider may be liable for violation of the individual's right to privacy, and the disclosure may be deemed a breach of confidentiality.

The "Needle Stick" Law

Since the advent of HIV/AIDS, there has been much concern among health care workers about needle stick injuries involving inappropriately discarded needles. Needle stick injuries can transfer blood and blood-borne pathogens , such as hepatitis B, hepatitis C, and HIV. Every year, there are over 500,000 accidental needle sticks, and more than 1,000 of those incidents lead to the HIV or hepatitis C virus infection.

For the past three years, the Service Employee International Union has lobbied on behalf of its members for legislation designed to prevent such needle stick injuries. Finally, in October 2000, lawmakers approved a bill that requires healthcare facilities to use retractable syringes to prevent needle stick injuries to health care workers.

INSURANCE COVERAGE

Although the insurance industry is not covered by the ADA, Congress has nevertheless stated that insurers will not be permitted to engage in practices that evade the purposes of the ADA. Some of the important concerns relating to both health and life insurance and the rights of the HIV-infected person are set forth below.

Health Insurance

The AIDS epidemic has caused an extraordinary burden on the health care system and, in turn, the health insurance business. Insurance companies have attempted to shield themselves from catastrophic losses by requiring applicants to undergo HIV testing. However, such requirements have been challenged with contrary results depending on the jurisdiction. Some jurisdictions have enacted legislation specifically prohibiting HIV testing and/or application questions designed to determine if the applicant is a member of a high-risk group.

Some jurisdictions have held that such requirements are nondiscriminatory and, in fact, sound insurance underwriting policies, particularly when underwriting a policy for an individual. The courts have permitted insurers to subject the individual applicant to more stringent requirements.

Nevertheless, when the policy in question is a large group policy, the courts have generally held that an HIV testing requirement is of "less certain validity" because the insurers are assessing risks characteristic of a group rather than a particular individual.

The Ryan White Care Act

In 1990, in an effort to ease the increased demand on the already over-burdened public health infrastructure due to the HIV/AIDS epidemic, the Legislature enacted the Ryan White Comprehensive AIDS Resources Emergency (CARE) Act. The Ryan White CARE Act represents the Federal Government's largest financial allocation specifically for HIV-related health and support services.

The CARE Act, which was reauthorized in 1996, provides funding to states and other public or private non-profit organizations to develop, organize, coordinate and operate more effective and cost-efficient systems for the delivery of essential health care and support services to medically underserved individuals and families affected by the HIV disease.

CARE Act funds are used to provide primary medical care, AIDS drugs, viral load testing, treatment information, support, case management, and other essential support services for tens of thousands of individuals living with HIV/AIDS. The CARE Act has dramatically improved the quality of life for people living with HIV and their families; reduced the use of costly impatient care; and increased access to care for underserved populations, including minority groups. The CARE Act has also reduced the need for expensive hospitalization or skilled nursing home care for people with AIDS.

Life Insurance

Underwriters of life insurance policies are similarly concerned with the HIV status of applicants. However, the impact on the life insurance industry is much less than the burden on the health insurance industry due to a number of factors:

1. There is an increased lifespan of HIV-infected individuals due to advancements in drug treatment;

2. The largest number of victims thus far have been among groups which are the least likely to purchase life insurance, e.g. minorities.

3. The availability of HIV testing during the application process; and

4. There are established insurance principles available to the insurer which will void a life insurance policy under certain conditions, e.g. if there has been material misrepresentation during the application process. For example, if an HIV-infected person denies having certain enumerated medical conditions on their application, when in fact he or she does suffer from such conditions, the life insurance policy would generally be unenforceable.

APPENDIX 1:
DIRECTORY OF STATE PHYSICIAN LICENSING BUREAUS

STATE	NAME	ADDRESS	TELEPHONE
Alabama,	Alabama State Board of Medical Examiners	P.O. Box 946, Montgomery, Alabama 36102	205-832-6890
Alaska	Alaska Board of Medical Examiners	Pouch D, Juneau, Alaska 99811	907-465-2541
Arizona	Arizona State Board of Medical Examiners	5060 North Nineteenth Avenue, Suite 300, Phoenix, Arizona 85015	602-255-3751
Arkansas	Arkansas State Medical Board	P.O. Box 102, Harrisburg, Arkansas 72432	501-578-2677
California	California Board of Medical Quality Assurance	1340 Howe Avenue, Sacramento, California 95825	916-920-6411
Colorado	Colorado Board of Medical Examiners	132 State Services Building, 1525 Sherman Street Denver, Colorado 80203	303-866-2468
Connecticut	Connecticut Medical Examining Board	79 Elm Street, Hartford, Connecticut 06115	203-566-5630
Delaware	Delaware Board of Medical Practice	Margaret O'Neill Building, P.O. Box 1401, Dover, Delaware 19901	302-763-4753

STATE	NAME	ADDRESS	TELEPHONE
District of Columbia	District of Columbia Commission on Licensure to Practice the Healing Ar,t	605 G Street N.W., Washington, DC 20001	202-727-5365
Florida	Florida Board of Medical Examiners	130 North Monroe Street, Tallahassee, Florida 32301	904-488-0595
Georgia	Georgia Composite Board of Medical Examiners	166 Pryor Street, Southwest Atlanta, Georgia 30303	404-656-7067
Hawaii	Hawaii Board of Medical Examiners	P.O. Box 3469, Honolulu, Hawaii 96801	808-548-4100
Idaho	Idaho State Board of Medicine	700 West State Street, Boise, Idaho 83720	208-334-2822
Illinois	Professional Regulation	106 West Randolph, Chicago, Illinois 60601	312-917-4500
Indiana	Medical Licensing Board of Indiana	One American Square, Suite 1020, P.O. Box 82067, Indianapolis, Indiana 46282	317-232-2960
Iowa	Iowa State Board of Medical Examiners	State Capitol Complex, Executive Hills West, Des Moines, Iowa 50319	515-281-5171
Kansas	Kansas State Board of Healing Arts	503 Kansas Avenue, Suite 500, Topeka, Kansas 66534	913-296-7413
Kentucky	Kentucky State Board of Medical Licensure	3532 Ephraim Drive, Louisville, Kentucky 40205	502-456-2220

STATE	NAME	ADDRESS	TELEPHONE
Louisiana	Louisiana State Board of Medical Examiners	830 Union Street, Suite 100, New Orleans, Louisiana 70112	504-524-6763
Maine	Maine State Board of Registration in Medicine	RFD #3, Box 461, Waterville, Maine 04901	207-873-2184
Maryland	Maryland Board of Medical Examiners	201 West Preston Street, Baltimore, Maryland 21201	301-383-2020
Massachusetts	Massachusetts Board of Registration in Medicine	Room 1511, Leverett Saltonstall Building, 100 Cambridge Street, Boston, Massachusetts 02202	617-727-9446
Michigan	Michigan Board of Medicine	905 Southland, P.O. Box 30018, Lansing, Michigan 48909	517-373-0680
Minnesota	Minnesota State Board of Medical Examiners	717 Delaware Street S.E., Suite 352, Minneapolis, Minnesota 55414	612-296-5534
Mississippi	Mississippi State Board of Medical Licensure	P.O. Box 1700, Jackson, Mississippi 39205	601-354-6645
Missouri	Missouri State Board of Registration for the Healing Arts	P.O. Box 4, Jefferson City, Missouri 65102	314-751-2334
Montana	Montana State Board of Medical Examiners	1424 9th Avenue, Helena, Montana 59620	406-449-3737
Nebraska	Nebraska Bureau of Examining Boards	P.O. Box 95007, Lincoln, Nebraska 68509	402-471-2115

STATE	NAME	ADDRESS	TELEPHONE
Nevada	Nevada State Board of Medical Examiners	P.O. Box 7238, Reno, Nevada 89510	702-329-2559
New Hampshire	New Hampshire Board of Registration in Medicine	Health and Welfare Building Hazen Drive, Concord, New Hampshire 03301	603-271-4502
New Jersey	New Jersey State Board of Medical Examiners	28 West State Street, Room 914, Trenton, New Jersey 08608	609-292-4843
New Mexico	New Mexico State Board of Medical Examiners	227 E. Palace Avenue, Santa Fe, New Mexico 87501	505-827-2215
New York	New York Department of Health Office of Professional Medical Conduct	Empire State Plaza, Tower Building, Albany, New York 12237	518-474-8537
North Carolina	North Carolina State Board of Medical Examiners	222 North Person Street, Suite 214, Raleigh, North Carolina 27601	919-833-5321
North Dakota	North Dakota Board of Medical Examiners	418 East Rosser Avenue, Bismarck, North Dakota 58501	701-233-9485
Ohio	Ohio State Medical Board	65 South Front Street, Suite 510, Columbus, Ohio 43215	614-466-3934
Oklahoma	Oklahoma State Board of Medical Examiners	P.O. Box 18256, Oklahoma City, Oklahoma 73154	405-848-6841
Oregon	Oregon Board of Medical Examiners	1002 Loyalty Building, 317 S.W. Alder Street, Portland, Oregon 97204	503-229-5770

STATE	NAME	ADDRESS	TELEPHONE
Pennsylvania	Pennsylvania Board of Medical Education and Licensure	P.O. Box 2649, Harrisburg, Pennsylvania 17105	717-787-2381
Rhode Island	Rhode Island Department of Health	104 Cannon Building, 75 Davis Street, Providence, Rhode Island 02908	401-277-2827
South Carolina	South Carolina State Board of Medical Examiners	1315 Blanding Street, Columbia, South Carolina 29201	803-758-3361
South Dakota	South Dakota State Board of Medical and Osteopathic Examiners	608 West Avenue, North Sioux Falls, South Dakota 57104	605-336-1965
Tennessee	Tennessee State Board of Medical Examiners	320 R.S. Gass State Office Building, Ben Allen Road, Nashville, Tennessee 37216	615-741-7280
Texas	Texas State Board of Medical Examiners	P.O. Box 13562, Capitol Station, Austin, Texas 78711	512-305-7010
Utah	Utah Department of Registration	State Office Building, Room 5000, Salt Lake City, Utah 84114	801-268-6242
Vermont	Vermont State Board of Medicine	109 State Street, Montpelier, Vermont 05602	802-828-2363
Virginia	Virginia State Board of Medicine	517 West Grace Street, Richmond, Virginia 23220	804-257-6497
Washington	Washington Department of Licensing	P.O. Box 9649, Olympia, Washington 98504	206-753-2205

STATE	NAME	ADDRESS	TELEPHONE
West Virginia	West Virginia Board of Medicine	3412B Chesterfield Avenue, Charleston, West Virginia 25304	304-348-2971
Wisconsin	Wisconsin Medical Examining Board	1400 East Washington Avenue, Madison, Wisconsin 53702	608-266-2811
Wyoming	Wyoming Board of Medical Examiners	Hathaway Building, 4th Floor, Cheyenne, Wyoming 82002	307-777-7120

APPENDIX 2: DIRECTORY OF STATE LICENSING AGENCIES FOR MEDICAL FACILITIES

STATE	NAME	DEPARTMENT	ADDRESS	TELEPHONE
Alabama	Alabama Department of Public Health	Health Facility Licensure and Certification	State Office Building, Montgomery, Alabama 36130	205-832-3253
Alaska	Department of Health and Social Services	Division of Public Health	Pouch H-06, Juneau, Alaska 99811	907-465-3090
Arizona	Department of Health	Health Facility Licensure and Certification	1740 West Adams Street, Phoenix, Arizona 85007	602-255-1118
Arkansas	Department of Health	Health Facility Services	4815 West Markham Street, Little Rock, Arkansas 72201	501-661-2201
California	Department of Health Services	Health Facilities Licensure and Certification	744 P Street, Sacramento, California 95814	916-445-3281
Colorado	Department of Health	Health Facility Licensure and Certification	4210 East Eleventh Avenue, Denver, Colorado 80220	303-320-8333

STATE	NAME	DEPARTMENT	ADDRESS	TELEPHONE
Connecticut	Department of Health Services	Hospital and Medical Care Services	79 Elm Street, Hartford, Connecticut 06115	203-566-3985
Delaware	Department of Health and Social Services	Health Facility Licensure and Certification	Jesse S. Cooper Memorial Building Dover, Delaware 19901	302-995-6674
District of Columbia	Department of Human Services	Health Facility Licensure and Certification	1875 Connecticut Avenue N.W., Washington, DC 20009	202-727-2009
Florida	Department of Health and Rehabilitative Services	Health Facility Licensure and Certification	1323 Winewood Boulevard, Tallahassee, Florida 32301	904-359-6022
Georgia	Department of Human Resources	Licensing and Certification	Atlanta, Georgia 30334	404-894-5144
Hawaii	Department of Health	Health Facility Licensure and Certification	Kinau Hale, P.O. Box 3378, Honolulu, Hawaii 96801	808-548-6510
Idaho	Department of Health and Welfare Division of Health	Health Facility Licensure and Certification	Statehouse Mail, Boise, Idaho 83720	208-334-4172
Illinois	Department of Public Health	Division of Health Facility Standards	525 West Jefferson, Springfield, Illinois 62761	217-782-7412

STATE	NAME	DEPARTMENT	ADDRESS	TELEPHONE
Indiana	Indiana State Board of Health	Health Facility Licensure and Certification	1330 West Michigan Street, P.O. Box 1964, Indianapolis, Indiana 46206	317-633-8442
Iowa	Department of Health	Health Facility Licensure and Certification	Lucas State Office Building, Des Moines, Iowa 50319	515-281-4125
Kansas	Department of Health and Environment	Health Facility Licensure and Certification	Forbes Field, Topeka, Kansas 66620	913-862-9360
Kentucky	Department of Human Resources	Ombudsman	275 Main Street, Frankfort, Kentucky 40621	502-564-5497
Louisiana	Department of Health and Human Resources	Office of Licensing and Regulations	P.O. Box 60630, New Orleans, Louisiana 70160	504-342-6721
Maine	Department of Human Services	Health Facility Licensure and Certification	Augusta, Maine 04333	207-289-2606
Maryland	Department of Health and Mental Hygiene	Licensing and Certification	201 West Preston Street, Baltimore, Maryland 21201	301-383-2517
Massachusetts	Office of Human Services	Health Facilities	600 Washington Street, Boston, Massachusetts 02111	617-727-6240

STATE	NAME	DEPARTMENT	ADDRESS	TELEPHONE
Michigan	Department of Public Health	Health Facility Licensing and Certification	3500 North Logan Street, Lansing, Michigan 48909	517-373-0900
Minnesota	Department of Health	Health Facility Licensure and Certification	717 Delaware Street S.E., Minneapolis, Minnesota 55440	612-296-5420
Mississippi	Health Care Commission	Health Facility Licensing and Certification	2688 Insurance Center Drive, Jackson, Mississippi 39201	601-981-6880
Missouri	Missouri Division of Health	Hospital Licensure and Certification	Broadway State Office Building, P.O. Box 570, Jefferson City, Missouri 65101	314-751-2713
Montana	Department of Health and Environmental Sciences	Health Facility Licensure and Certification	Cogswell Building, Helena, Montana 59620	406-449-2037
Nebraska	Department of Health	Health Facility Licensure and Certification	301 Centennial Mall South, Lincoln, Nebraska 68509	402-471-2105
Nevada	Department of Human Resources	Health Facility Licensure and Certification	505 East King Street - Capitol Complex, Carson City, Nevada 89710	702-884-4475

STATE	NAME	DEPARTMENT	ADDRESS	TELEPHONE
New Hampshire	Division of Public Health Services	Health Facility Licensure and Certification, Health and Welfare Building	Hazen Drive, Concord, New Hampshire 03301	603-271-4592
New Jersey	Department of Health	Health Facility Licensure and Certification	CN 360, John Fitch Plaza, Trenton, New Jersey 08625	609-292-5764
New Mexico	Health and Environment Department	Bureau of Health Facilities	P.O. Box 968, Santa Fe, New Mexico 87504	505-827-2745
New York	Department of Health Bureau of Project Management	Division of Health Facility Planning	Corning Tower, Suite 9-300, Empire State Plaza, Albany, New York 12237	518-473-4119
North Carolina	Department of Human Resources Division of Health Services	Health Facility Licensure and Certification	P.O. Box 2091, Raleigh, North Carolina 27602	919-733-2342
North Dakota	State Department of Health	Health Facility Licensure and Certification	State Capitol, Bismarck, North Dakota 58505	701-224-2352
Ohio	Department of Health	Health Facility Licensure and Certification	P.O. Box 118, Columbus, Ohio 43216	614-466-7857
Oklahoma	State Department of Health	Health Facilities Service	P.O. Box 53551, Oklahoma City, Oklahoma 73152	405-271-5114

STATE	NAME	DEPARTMENT	ADDRESS	TELEPHONE
Oregon	Department of Human Resources	Health Facility Licensure and Certification	P.O. Box 231, Portland, Oregon 97207	503-229-5686
Pennsylvania	Department of Health	Hospital Licensing	P.O. Box 90, Harrisburg, Pennsylvania 17120	717-783-8980
Rhode Island	Department of Health	Facility Regulation	75 Davis Street, Providence, Rhode Island 02908	401-277-2566
South Carolina	Department of Health and Environmental Control	Health Facility Licensing and Certification	2600 Bull Street, Columbia, South Carolina 29201	803-758-4567
South Dakota	Department of Health	Health Facility Licensure and Certification	Joe Foss Building, Pierre, South Dakota 57501	605-773-3364
Tennessee	Department of Public Health	Health Facility Licensure and Certification	Cordell Hull Building, Nashville, Tennessee 37219	615-741-6379
Texas	Department of Health	Bureau of Licensing and Certification	1100 West 49th Street, Austin, Texas 78756	512-458-7538
Utah	Utah Department of Health	Health Facility Licensure and Certification	150 West North Temple, P.O. Box 2500, Salt Lake City, Utah 84110	801-533-7016

STATE	NAME	DEPARTMENT	ADDRESS	TELEPHONE
Vermont	Department of Health	Health Facility Licensure and Certification	60 Main Street, Burlington, Vermont 05401	802-862-5701
Virginia	State Health Department	Health Facility Licensing and Certification	109 Governor Street, Richmond, Virginia 23219	804-786-2081
Washington	Department of Social and Health Services	Health Facility Licensure and Certification	Mail Stop LJ-18, Olympia, Washington 98504	206-753-5851
West Virginia	Department of Health	Health Facilities Evaluation	State Capitol Complex, Charleston, West Virginia 25305	304-348-0530
Wisconsin	Division of Health	Health Facility Licensing and Certification	P.O. Box 309, Madison, Wisconsin 53701	608-266-2055
Wyoming	Health and Medical Services	Health Facility Licensure and Certification	Hathaway Building, Cheyenne, Wyoming 82002	307-777-7120

APPENDIX 3: SAMPLE INFORMED CONSENT AGREEMENT

I, [name of patient] allow [name of physician] to perform upon me an operation known as [type of operation to be performed, e.g., appendectomy, mastectomy, etc.]. I further understand that he/she may be assisted in performing this operation by [list any assisting physicians, if applicable], but that the operation will be primarily performed by [name of physician].

I have been informed that [name of physician] has performed [#] [type of operation[s]] during the last 12 months and that the mortality rate was [xx%], the infection rate was [xx%] and the mistake rate was [xx%].

The hospital, [name of physician], has informed me that [#] related operations were performed during the last 12 months at this facility and that the mortality rate was [xx%], the infection rate was [xx%], and the mistake rate was [xx%].

Dr. [name of physician] and this hospital carry liability insurance in the amount of [$xxx] and [$xxx] respectively. This liability insurance is/is not approximately the same as other doctors and hospitals performing this operation would be expected to carry to provide compensation to patients who may die or be injured by medical mismanagement.

I have been informed that a [type of operation] is a major/minor operation and will be performed as described below:

[Describe in detail procedure to be performed as well as the physician's rights to perform further surgery if an unexpected condition is encountered during the course of the surgery].

As with any major surgery, bleeding can occur and at times can be serious. In addition, infection can occur and the risks of developing such an infection are as reported above. [Describe all further risks of the procedure in detail].

[Describe details of recovery period].

I have been advised that a [type of operation] is necessary because [provide details as to why the particular procedure is necessary].

I have been advised that the alternatives of treatment include [provide details of all alternative treatments available, including the possible outcome and risks associated with the alternative treatments].

I have been advised that it is the opinion of my doctor that a [type of operation] is indicated and the risks of the operation are less than the alternatives, and I have been given the opportunity of seeking independent consultation prior to having this surgery.

Although I have been fully informed about the risks of undergoing a [type of procedure], I am willing to undergo the operation. This does not relieve my doctor of any responsibilities for acts of negligence, which would include rendering substandard care to me, causing injuries which should not have occurred, even though I am aware that there may be a risk in having the operation performed. I agree to undergo a [type of operation] after being fully informed, but expect that proper care shall be rendered to me at all times. This includes post-operative care by my physicians and the nurses and hospital personnel.

Dated: ______________________

____

Signature Line for Patient

Dated: ______________________

____

Signature Line for Doctor

APPENDIX 4: RELEASE FROM LIABILITY FOR DISCONTINUING LIFE-SUSTAINING PROCEDURES

We, the undersigned, are the family of [name of patient] . [His or her] attending physician [name of physician] has advised that [patient] has suffered severe and irreversible brain injury that precludes any cognitive, meaningful or functional future existence. [Note: Or set forth a similar statement of the patient's condition].

We understand that [his or her] current survival is contingent upon [insert the procedure to be withheld or withdrawn]. It is our desire and that of the patient as expressed in [his or her] Living Will, Health Care Declaration, Durable Power of Attorney, and/or Appointment of Health Care Agent executed on [date[s]], that all "life-sustaining procedures" as therein defined be discontinued.

By [my or our] signature(s), we hereby release and agree to hold harmless [his or her] physicians and the nurses and staff of [name of facility], from any liability, claims for damages, or causes of action that might otherwise be brought as a result of the death that likely will occur subsequent to the discontinuance of the above-described life-sustaining procedures.

[Insert Date]

BY: [Insert signature line for Name/Address of Guardian, Next of Kin, Proxy or Surrogate as Releasor] ______________________________

____

[State relationship to patient]

____

BY: [Witness #1]

[Insert Date] ______________________

____

BY: [Witness #1]

____

[Insert Date]

Subscribed and acknowledged before me by the Releasor [Insert Name of Releasor], and by [Insert Names of Witnesses], the Witnesses, this day of ________________ , 20 __.

[Notary Stamp]

APPENDIX 5: SAMPLE LIVING WILL

DECLARATION made this (enter date) _______________.

I, (Name and address), being of sound mind, willfully and voluntarily make known my desire that my life shall not be artificially prolonged under the circumstances set forth below, and do hereby declare:

MEDICAL CONDITION

1. If at any time I should have a terminal or incurable condition caused by injury, disease, or illness, certified to be terminal or incurable by at least two physicians, which within reasonable medical judgment would cause my death, and where the application of life-sustaining procedures would serve only to artificially prolong the moment of my death, I direct that such procedures be withheld or withdrawn, and that I be permitted to die with dignity.

2. If at any time I experience irreversible brain injury, or a disease, illness, or condition that results in my being in a permanent, irreversible vegetative or comatose state, and such injury, disease, illness, or condition would preclude any cognitive, meaningful, or functional future existence, I direct my physicians and any other attending nursing or health care personnel to allow me to die with dignity, even if that requires the withdrawal or withholding of nutrition or hydration and my death will follow such withdrawal or withholding.

LIFE-SUSTAINING PROCEDURES

It is my expressed intent that the term "life-sustaining procedures" shall include not only medical or surgical procedures or interventions that utilize mechanical or other artificial means to sustain, restore, or supplant a vital function, but also shall include the placement, withdrawal, withholding, or maintenance of nasogastric tubes, gastrostomy, intravenous lines, or any other artificial, surgical, or invasive means for nutritional support and/or hydration.

"Life-sustaining procedures" shall not be interpreted to include the administration of medication or the performance of any medical procedure deemed necessary to provide routine care and comfort or alleviate pain.

RIGHT TO REFUSE TREATMENT

It is my intent and expressed desire that this Declaration shall be honored by my family, physicians, nurses, and any other attending health care personnel as the final expression of my constitutional and legal right to refuse medical or surgical treatment and to accept the consequences of such refusal. Any ambiguities, questions, or uncertainties that might arise in the reading, interpretation, or implementation of this Declaration shall be resolved in a manner to give complete expression to my legal right to refuse treatment and shall be construed as clear and convincing evidence of my intentions and desires.

REVOCATION OF PREVIOUSLY EXECUTED DOCUMENTS

I understand the full importance of this Declaration and I am emotionally and mentally competent to make this Declaration, and by my execution, I hereby revoke any previously executed Health Care Declaration.

COPIES AND DISTRIBUTION

The original of this document is kept at (address where kept). I have made (#) copies of this document. Numbered and signed copies have been provided to the following individuals or institutions: (List names, addresses and phone numbers of individuals and institutions).

STATEMENT OF WITNESSES

I state this (enter date), under penalty of perjury, that the Declarant has identified (himself or herself) to me and that the Declarant signed or acknowledged this Health Care Declaration in my presence.

I believe the Declarant to be of sound mind, and the Declarant has affirmed (his or her) awareness of the nature of this document and is signing it voluntarily and free from duress. The Declarant requested that I serve as a witness to (his or her) execution of this document.

I declare that I am not related to the Declarant by blood, marriage, or adoption and that to the best of my knowledge I am not entitled to any part of the estate of the Declarant on the death of the principal under a will or by operation of law.

I am not a provider of health or residential care, an employee of a provider of health or residential care, the operator of a community care facility, or an employee of an operator of a health care facility.

I declare that I have no claim against any portion of the estate of the Declarant upon (his or her) death, nor any personal financial responsibility for the payment of Declarant's medical bills or any other of Declarant's obligations.

____
Signature Line of Witness #1

____
Address of Witness #1

____
Signature Line of Witness #2

____
Address of Witness #2

____
Signature Line of Witness #3

____
Address of Witness #3

Subscribed and acknowledged before me by the Declarant, (Name), and by his or her Witnesses (Names) _________________________ on (enter date) ___________________ .

Notary Signature and Stamp

APPENDIX 6: TABLE OF STATE LIVING WILL STATUTES

STATE	STATUTE	SECTION
Alabama	Natural Death Act	Code of Alabama §22-8A-1 et seq.
Alaska	Rights of Terminally Ill Act	Alaska Statutes §18.12.010 et seq.
Arizona	Medical Treatment Decision Act	Arizona Revised Statutes §36-3261
Arkansas	Rights of the Terminally Ill or Permanently Unconscious Act	Arkansas Statutes Annotated §20-17-201 et seq.
California	Natural Death Act	California Health & Safety Code §7188
Colorado	Medical Treatment Decision Act	Colorado Revised Statutes §15-18-101
Connecticut	Removal of Life Support Systems Connecticut	General Statutes Annotated §19a-570 et seq.
Delaware	Delaware Death with Dignity Act	Delaware Code Annotated Title 16 §2501 et seq.
District of Columbia	Natural Death Act	District of Columbia Code Title 6 §2421 et seq.
Florida	Life Prolonging Procedure Act	Florida Statutes Annotated §765.101 et seq.
Georgia	Living Wills Act	Code of Georgia §31-32-1
Hawaii	Medical Treatment Decisions Act	Hawaii Revised Statutes §327D
Idaho	Natural Death Act	Idaho Code §39-4501 et seq.

STATE	STATUTE	SECTION
Illinois	Living Will Act	Illinois Revised Statutes Chapter 110-1/2 §701 et seq.
Indiana	Living Wills and Life Prolonging Procedures Act	Indiana Code Annotated §16-8-11-1 et seq.
Iowa	Life Sustaining Procedures Act	Code of Iowa §144A.
Kansas	Natural Death Act	Kansas Statutes Annotated §65-28103(a) e. seq.
Kentucky	Living Will Act	Kentucky Revised Statutes §311.624 et seq.
Louisiana	Natural Death Act	Louisiana Revised Statutes §40:1299.58.
Maine	Living Will Act	Maine Revised Statutes Annotated Title 18-A §5-701 et seq.
Maryland	Life Sustaining Procedures Act	Maryland Health General Code Annotated §5-601 et seq.
Massachusetts	No statutory provision	
Michigan	No statutory provision	
Minnesota	Adult Health Care Decisions Act	Minnesota Statutes §145B.03 et seq.
Mississippi	Natural Death Act	Mississippi Code Annotated41-41-105 et seq.
Missouri	Life Support Declaration	Annotated Missouri Statutes §459.010 et seq.
Montana	Living Will Act	Revised Montana Code Annotated §50-9-101 et seq.
Nebraska	No statutory provision	
Nevada	Living Will Statute	Nevada Revised Statutes §449.600
New Hampshire	Terminal Care Document	New Hampshire Revised Statutes Annotated 137-H §§1-16

STATE	STATUTE	SECTION
New Jersey	Living Will Statute	New Jersey Statutes Annotated Chapter 201
New Mexico	Right to Die Act	New Mexico Statutes Annotated §24-7-1 et seq.
New York	No statutory provision	
North Carolina	Natural Death Act	General Statutes of North Carolina §90-320 et seq.
North Dakota	Uniform Rights of Terminally Ill Act	North Dakota Century Code §23-06.4
Ohio	Living Will Statute	Ohio Revised Code Annotated §2133.01 et seq.
Oklahoma	Natural Death Act	Oklahoma Statutes Annotated §663-3101.1 et seq.
Oregon	Directive to Physicians	Oregon Revised Statutes §127.610 et seq.
Pennsylvania	No statutory provision	
Rhode Island	No statutory provision	
South Carolina	Death with Dignity Act	Code of Laws of South Carolina §44-77-10 et seq.
South Dakota	Living Will Statute	South Dakota Codified Laws Annotated §34-12D
Tennessee	Right to Natural Death Act	Tennessee Code Annotated §32-11-101 et seq.
Texas	Natural Death Act	Texas Revised Civil Statutes Annotated §672.004 et seq.
Utah	Personal Choice and Living Will Act	Utah Code Annotated §75-2-1101 et seq.
Vermont	Terminal Care Document	Vermont Statutes Annotated Title 18 §5251
Virginia	Natural Death Act	Code of Virginia Annotated §54.1-2981 et seq.
Washington	Natural Death Act	Washington Revised Code Annotated §70-122.010 et seq.

STATE	STATUTE	SECTION
West Virginia	Natural Death Act	West Virginia Code Chapter 16 Article 30 et seq.
Wisconsin	Natural Death Act	Wisconsin Statutes Annotated §154.01 et seq.
Wyoming	Living Will Act	Wyoming Statutes 35-22-102 et seq.

APPENDIX 7: SAMPLE DURABLE POWER OF ATTORNEY FOR HEALTH CARE

APPOINTMENT made this (enter date) ______________________.

I, ________________________(Name and address), being of sound mind, willfully and voluntarily appoint (name, address, city, state, phone), as my Health Care Agent (hereinafter "Agent") with a Durable Power of Attorney to make any and all health care decisions for me, except to the extent stated otherwise in this document.

EFFECTIVE DATE

This Durable Power of Attorney and Appointment of Health Care Agent shall take effect at such time as I become comatose, incapacitated, or otherwise mentally or physically incapable of giving directions or consent regarding the use of life-sustaining procedures or any other health care measures.

"Health care" in this context means any treatment, service, or procedure utilized to maintain, diagnose, or treat any physical or mental condition.

DETERMINATION OF MEDICAL CONDITION

A determination of incapacity shall be certified by my attending physician and by a second physician who is neither employed by the facility where I am a patient nor associated in practice with my attending physician and who shall be appointed to independently assess and evaluate my capacity by the appropriate administrator of the facility where I am a patient.

AUTHORITY OF HEALTH CARE AGENT

My Agent is authorized, in consultation with my attending physician, to direct the withdrawal or withholding of any life-sustaining procedures, as defined herein, as (he or she) solely in the exercise of (his or her) judgment shall determine are appropriate to give comply with my wishes and desires.

In addition, my Agent by acceptance of this Appointment agrees and is hereby directed to use (his or her) best efforts to make those decisions that I would make in the exercise of my right to refuse treatment and not those that (he or she) or others might believe to be in my best interests.

APPOINTMENT OF ALTERNATE AGENTS

If the person designated as my Agent is unable or unwilling to accept this Appointment, I designate the following persons to serve as my Agent to make health care decisions for me as authorized by this document. They shall serve in the following order:

1. First Alternate Agent: (name, address and telephone)
2. Second Alternate Agent: (name, address and telephone)

DURATION

I understand that this Power of Attorney exists indefinitely unless I define a shorter time herein or execute a revocation. If I am incapacitated at such time as this Power of Attorney expires (if applicable), the authority I have granted my Agent shall continue until such time as I am capable of giving directions regarding my health care.

(If applicable:) This power of attorney ends on the following date:

COPIES AND DISTRIBUTION

The original of this document is kept at (address where kept). I have made (#) copies of this document. Numbered and signed copies have been provided to the following individuals or institutions: (List names, addresses and phone numbers of individuals and institutions).

STATEMENT OF WITNESSES

I state this (enter date), under penalty of perjury, that the Declarant has identified (himself or herself) to me and that the Declarant signed or acknowledged this Durable Power of Attorney and Appointment of Health Care Agent in my presence.

I believe the Declarant to be of sound mind, and the Declarant has affirmed (his or her) awareness of the nature of this document and is signing it voluntarily and free from duress. The Declarant requested that I serve as a witness to (his or her) execution of this document.

I am not the person appointed as Agent by this document, and I am not a provider of health or residential care, an employee of a provider of health or residential care, the operator of a community care facility, or an employee of an operator of a health care facility.

I declare that I am not related to the Declarant by blood, marriage, or adoption and that to the best of my knowledge I am not entitled to any part of the estate of the Declarant on the death of the principal under a will or by operation of law.

I declare that I have no claim against any portion of the estate of the Declarant upon (his or her) death, nor any personal financial responsibility for the payment of Declarant's medical bills or any other of Declarant's obligations.

____
Signature Line of Witness #1

____
Address of Witness #1

____
Signature Line of Witness #2

____
Address of Witness #2

____
Signature Line of Witness #3

____
Address of Witness #3

Subscribed and acknowledged before me by the Declarant, (Name), and by his or her witnesses (Names) on (enter date).

Notary Signature and Stamp

APPENDIX 8: THE AMA STATEMENT ON WITHHOLDING OR WITHDRAWING OF LIFE-PROLONGING MEDICAL TREATMENT

The social commitment of the physician is to sustain life and relieve suffering. Where the performance of one duty conflicts with the other, the choice of the patient, or his family or legal representative if the patient is incompetent to act in his own behalf, should prevail. In the absence of the patient's choice or an authorized proxy, the physician must act in the best interest of the patient.

For humane reasons, with informed consent, a physician may do what is medically necessary to alleviate severe pain, or cease or omit treatment to permit a terminally ill patient whose death is imminent to die. However, he should not intentionally cause death. In deciding whether the administration of potentially life-prolonging medical treatment is in the best interest of the patient who is incompetent to act in his own behalf, the physician should determine what the possibility is for extending life under humane and comfortable conditions and what are the prior expressed wishes of the patient and attitudes of the family or those who have responsibility for the custody of the patient.

Even if death is not imminent but a patient's coma is beyond doubt irreversible and there are adequate safeguards to confirm the accuracy of the diagnosis and with the concurrence of those who have responsibility for the care of the patient, it is not unethical to discontinue all means of life-prolonging medical treatment.

Life-prolonging medical treatment includes medication and artificially or technologically supplied respiration, nutrition or hydration. In treating a terminally ill or irreversibly comatose patient, the physician should determine whether the benefits of treatment outweigh its burdens. At all times, the dignity of the patient should be maintained.

APPENDIX 9: SAMPLE DO NOT RESUSCITATE ORDER ("DNR ORDER")

Name: ______________________

Date of Birth: ______________________

DO NOT RESUSCITATE THE PERSON NAMED ABOVE. IF IN CARDIAC ARREST, THE INDIVIDUAL NAMED ABOVE IS TO RECEIVE NO CARDIOPULMONARY RESUSCITATION (CPR), NO ELECTRIC DEFIBRILLATION, NO TRACHEAL INTUBATION, AND NO VENTILATORY ASSISTANCE.

Effective Date: ______________________

Physician's Signature: ______________________

Print Physician's Name: ______________________

CONSENT

I understand that this document is a Do Not Resuscitate Order. I further understand that, in the event of suffering cardiac arrest, I am refusing cardiopulmonary resuscitation in situations where death may be imminent. I make this request knowingly and I am aware of the alternatives. I expressly release, on behalf of myself and my family, all persons who shall in the future attend to my medical care of any and all liability whatsoever for acting in accordance with this request.

Furthermore, I direct that these guidelines be enforced even though I may develop a diminished mental capacity in the future. I am aware that I may revoke these instructions at any time by (1) the physical destruction or verbal rescinding of this order by the physician who signed it; or (2) by the physical destruction or verbal rescinding of this order by the person who gave written informed consent to the order, including myself or my legally authorized guardian, agent, or surrogate decision maker.

[Authorized signature of patient or patient's health care agent, surrogate decision maker or legal guardian]

APPENDIX 10: NATIONAL DIRECTORY OF ORGANIZATIONS SUPPORTING CHOICE FOR TERMINALLY ILL PATIENTS

NAME	ADDRESS	TELEPHONE
Americans for Death with Dignity	1783 Terrace Drive, Belmont, CA 94002	415-593-28631
Center for Social Gerentology	117 No. 1st Street, Suite 204, Ann Arbor, MI 48104	313-665-1126
Choice in Dying	475 Riverside Drive, Room 1852, New York, NY 10115	212-870-2003
Compassion in Dying	6312 S.W. Capitol Highway, Suite 415, Portland, OR 97201	503-221-9556
Death with Dignity Education Center	520 El Camino Real, Suite 710, San Mateo, CA 94402-1720	415-344-6489
Dying Well Network	P.O. Box 880, Spokane, WA 99210	509-926-2457
Euthanasia Research & Guidance Organization (ERGO)	24829 Norris Lane, Junction City, Oregon 97448-9559	541-998-1873
Hemlock Society USA	P.O. Box 101810, Denver, CO 80250	303-639-1202 Life-Fax
IDR Technology Inc.	P.O. Box 501136, Atlanta, GA 31150	404-696-0377
Legal Counsel for the Elderly	1909 K Street N.W., Washington, DC 20049	N/A

NAME	ADDRESS	TELEPHONE
Legal Services for the Elderly	132 W. 43rd Street, 3rd Floor, New York, NY 10036	212-595-1340
Merian's Friends	P.O. Box 272, Northville, MI 48167	888-217-0700
National Health Law Program	2639 S. La Cienega Blvd., Los Angeles, CA 90034	213-204-6010
National Health Law Program	2025 M Street N.W., Washington, DC 20036	202-887-5310
National Senior Citizens Law Center	1052 W. 6th Street, 7th Floor, Los Angeles, CA 90017	213-482-3550
National Senior Citizens Law Center	2025 M Street N.W, Suite 400, Washington, DC 20036	202-887-5280

APPENDIX 11: DIRECTORY OF STATE OFFICES OF LONG-TERM CARE OMBUDSMAN

NAME	ADDRESS	TELEPHONE NUMBER
Alabama	Commission on Aging, 136 Catoma Street 2nd Floor, Montgomery, AL 36130	205-242-5743
Alaska	Office of the Older Alaskans Ombudsman, 3601 C Street, Suite 260, Anchorage, AK 99503	907-279-2232
Arizona	Aging and Adult Administration,1400 West Washington Street, Phoenix, AZ 85005	602-542-4446
Arkansas	Arkansas State Office on Aging, 1417 Donaghey Plaza South, Little Rock, AR 72203	501-682-8952
California	Department of Aging, 1600 K Street, Sacramento, CA 95814	916-322-6681
Colorado	Aging and Adult Services Division, 455 Sherman Street, Denver, CO 80203	303-722-0300
Connecticut	Department on Aging, 175 Main Street, Hartford, CT 06106	203-566-7770
Delaware	Division of Aging, 1113 Church Avenue, Milford, DE 19963	302-422-1386
District of Columbia	Office on Aging, 1909 K Street N.W., Washington, DC 20049	202-833-6720
Florida	Program Office of Aging and Adult Services, 154 Holland Avenue, Tallahassee, FL 32399	904-488-6190
Georgia	Office of Aging, 878 Peachtree Street N.E., Room 632, Atlanta, GA 30309	404-894-5336

NAME	ADDRESS	TELEPHONE NUMBER
Hawaii	Executive Office on Aging, 335 Merchant Street, Room 241, Honolulu, HI 96813	808-548-2539
Idaho	Office on Aging, State House, Room 114, Boise, ID 83720	208-334-3833
Illinois	Department on Aging,421 East Capitol Avenue, Springfield, IL 62706	217-785-3140
Indiana	Department on Aging & Community Services, 251 N. Illinois Street, Indianapolis, IN 46204	317-232-7020
Iowa	Commission on Aging, 914 Grand Avenue, Suite 236, Jewett Building, Des Moines, IA 50319	515-281-5187
Kansas	Department of Aging, 915 Southwest Harrison, Topeka, KS 66612	913-296-4986
Kentucky	Division for Aging Services, 275 East Main Street, 6th Floor, Frankfort, KY 40601	502-564-6930
Louisiana	Office of Elderly Affairs, 4528 Bennington Avenue, LA 70898	504-925-1700
Maine	Commission on Aging, State House, Station No. 127, Augusta, ME 04333	207-289-3658
Maryland	Office on Aging, 301 West Preston Street, Baltimore, MD 21201	301-225-1083
Massachusetts	Department of Elder Affairs, 38 Chauncy Street, Boston, MA 02111	617-727-7273
Michigan	Citizens for Better Care, 1627 East Kalamazoo, Lansing, MI 48912	517-482-1297
Minnesota	Office of Ombudsman for Older Minnesotans, 444 Lafayette Road, St. Paul, MN 55155	612-296-3969
Mississippi	Mississippi Council on Aging, 421 West Pascagoula Street, Jackson, MS 39203	601-949-2070
Missouri	Division on Aging, 2701 West Main Street, Jefferson City, MO 65102	314-751-3082

NAME	ADDRESS	TELEPHONE NUMBER
Montana	Seniors' Office of Legal and Ombudsman Services, P.O. Box 232, Capitol Station, Helena, MT 59620	406-444-4676
Nebraska	Department on Aging, 301 Centennial Mall South, Lincoln, NE 68509	402-471-2306
Nevada	Division of Aging Services, 340 North 11th Street, Suite 114, Las Vegas, NV 89101	702-486-3545
New Hampshire	Division of Elderly and Adult Services, 6 Hazen Drive, Concord, NH 03301	603-271-4375
New Jersey	Office of the Ombudsman for the Institutionalized Elderly, 28 West State Street, Room 305, Trenton, NJ 08625	609-292-8016
New Mexico	State Agency on Aging, 224 East Palace Avenue, 4th Floor, Santa Fe, NM 87501	505-827-7640
New York	Office for the Aging, Empire State Plaza, Agency Building No. 2, Albany, NY 12223	518-474-7329
North Carolina	Division of Aging, 693 Palmer Drive, Raleigh, NC 27603	919-733-8400
North Dakota	Aging Services, State Capitol Building, Bismarck, ND 58505	701-224-2577
Ohio	Department of Aging, 50 West Broad Street, 9th Floor, Columbus, OH 43215	614-466-9927
Oklahoma	Special Unit on Aging, P.O. Box 25352, Oklahoma City, OK 73125	405-521-6734
Oregon	Office of Long-Term Care Ombudsman, 2475 Lancaster Drive, Building B, Number 9, Salem, OR 97310	503-378-6533
Pennsylvania	Department of Aging, 231 State Street, Harrisburg, PA 17120	717-783-7247
Rhode Island	Department of Elderly Affairs, 160 Pine Street, Providence, RI 02903	401-277-6883

NAME	ADDRESS	TELEPHONE NUMBER
South Carolina	Division of Ombudsman and Citizens' Service, 1205 Pendleton Street, Columbia, SC 29201	803-734-0457
South Dakota	Office of Adult Services and Aging, 700 North Illinois Street, Pierre, SD 57501	605-773-3656
Tennessee	Commission on Aging, 706 Church Street, Suite 201, Nashville, TN 37243	615-741-2056
Texas	Department on Aging, P.O. Box 12786, Capitol Station, Austin, TX 78741	512-444-2727
Utah	Division of Aging and Adult Services, 120 North - 200 West, Box 45500, Salt Lake City, UT 84145	801-538-3924
Vermont	Office on Aging, 103 South Main Street, Waterbury, VT 05676	802-241-2400
Virginia	Office on Aging, 700 East Franklin Street, Richmond, VA 23219	804-225-2271
Washington	South King County Multi-Service Center, 1200 S. 336 Street, Federal Way, Olympia, WA 98003	206-838-6810
West Virginia	Commission on Aging, State Capitol, Charleston, WV 25305	304-558-3317
Wisconsin	Board on Aging and Long Term Care, 214 North Hamilton Street, Madison, WI 53703	608-266-8944
Wyoming	State Bar Association, 900 8th Street, Wheatland, WY 82201	307-322-5553

APPENDIX 12: SELECTED PROVISIONS OF THE MEDICAL INFORMATION PRIVACY AND SECURITY ACT (S. 573)

SECTION 1. SHORT TITLE; TABLE OF CONTENTS.

(a) SHORT TITLE—This Act may be cited as the `Medical Information Privacy and Security Act'.

(b) TABLE OF CONTENTS [omitted]

SECTION 2. FINDINGS.

The Congress finds as follows:

(1) Individuals have a right of privacy with respect to their protected health information and records.

(2) With respect to information about medical care and health status, the traditional right of confidentiality (between a health care provider and a patient) is at risk.

(3) An erosion of the right of privacy may reduce the willingness of patients to confide in physicians and other practitioners and may inhibit patients from seeking care.

(4) An individual's privacy right means that the individual's consent is needed to disclose his or her protected health information and that the individual has a right of access to that health information.

(5) Any disclosure of protected health information should be limited to that information or portion of the medical record necessary to fulfill the immediate and specific purpose of the disclosure.

(6) Health research often depends on access to both identifiable and de—identified patient health information and health research is critically important to the health and well—being of all people in the United States.

(7) The Supreme Court found in Jaffee v. Redmond (116 S.Ct. 1923 (1996)) that there is an imperative need for confidence and trust between a psychotherapist and a patient and that such trust can only be established by an assurance of confidentiality. This assurance serves the public interest by facilitating the provision of appropriate treatment for individuals.

(8) Section 264 of the Health Insurance Portability and Accountability Act of 1996 (42 U.S.C. 1320d—2 note) establishes a deadline that Congress enact legislation, before August 21, 1999, to protect the privacy of protected health information.

SECTION 3. PURPOSES.

The purposes of this Act are as follows:

(1) To recognize that there is a right to privacy with respect to health information, including genetic information, and that this right must be protected.

(2) To create incentives to turn protected health information into de—identified health information, where appropriate.

(3) To designate an Office of Health Information Privacy within the Department of Health and Human Services to protect that right of privacy.

(4) To provide individuals with——

(A) access to health information of which they are the subject; and

(B) the opportunity to challenge the accuracy and completeness of such information by being able to file supplements to such information.

(5) To provide individuals with the right to limit the use and disclosure of protected health information.

(6) To establish strong and effective mechanisms to protect against the unauthorized and inappropriate use of protected health information.

(7) To invoke the sweep of congressional powers, including the power to enforce the 14th amendment, to regulate commerce, and to abrogate the immunity of the States under the 11th amendment, in order to address violations of the rights of individuals to privacy, to provide individuals with access to their health information, and to

prevent unauthorized use of protected health information that is genetic information.

(8) To establish strong and effective remedies for violations of this Act.

(9) To protect the rights of States.

SECTION 4. DEFINITIONS. [OMITTED]

TITLE I——INDIVIDUALS' RIGHTS

SUBTITLE A——ACCESS TO PROTECTED HEALTH INFORMATION BY SUBJECTS OF THE INFORMATION

SECTION 101. INSPECTION AND COPYING OF PROTECTED HEALTH INFORMATION.

(a) RIGHT OF INDIVIDUAL—

(1) IN GENERAL—A health care provider, health plan, employer, health or life insurer, school, or university, or a person acting as the agent of any such person, shall permit an individual who is the subject of protected health information, or the individual's designee, to inspect and copy protected health information concerning the individual, including records created under sections 102, 112, 202, 203, 208, and 211, that such person maintains.

(2) PROCEDURES AND FEES—A person described in paragraph (1) may set forth appropriate procedures to be followed for inspection and copying under such paragraph and may require an individual to pay fees associated with such inspection and copying in an amount that is not in excess of the actual costs of providing such copying. Such fees may not be assessed where such an assessment would have the effect of inhibiting an individual from gaining access to the information described in paragraph (1).

(b) DEADLINE—A person described in subsection (a)(1) shall comply with a request for inspection or copying of protected health information under this section not later than 15 business days after the date on which the person receives the request.

(c) RULES GOVERNING AGENTS—A person acting as the agent of a person described in subsection (a) shall provide for the inspection and copying of protected health information if——

(1) the protected health information is retained by the agent; and

(2) the agent has been asked by the person involved to fulfill the requirements of this section.

(d) SPECIAL RULE RELATING TO ONGOING CLINICAL TRIALS—With respect to protected health information that is created as part of an individual's participation in an ongoing clinical trial, access to the information shall be provided consistent with the individual's agreement to participate in the clinical trial.

SECTION 102. SUPPLEMENTS TO PROTECTED HEALTH INFORMATION.

(a) IN GENERAL—Not later than 45 days after the date on which a health care provider, health plan, employer, health or life insurer, school, or university, or a person acting as the agent of any such person, receives from an individual a request in writing to supplement protected health information concerning the individual, such person——

(1) shall add the supplement requested to the information;

(2) shall inform the individual that the supplement has been made; and

(3) shall make reasonable efforts to inform any person to whom the portion of the unsupplemented information was previously disclosed, of any substantive supplement that has been made.

(b) REFUSAL TO SUPPLEMENT—If a person described in subsection (a) declines to make the supplement requested under such subsection, the person shall inform the individual in writing of——

(1) the reasons for declining to make the supplement;

(2) any procedures for further review of the declining of such supplement; and

(3) the individual's right to file with the person a concise statement setting forth the requested supplement and the individual's reasons for disagreeing with the declining person and the individual's right to include a copy of this refusal in his or her health record.

(c) STATEMENT OF DISAGREEMENT—If an individual has filed with a person a statement of disagreement under subsection (b)(3), the person, in any subsequent disclosure of the disputed portion of the information——

(1) shall include, at the individual's request, a copy of the individual's statement; and

(2) may include a concise statement of the reasons for not making the requested supplement.

(d) RULES GOVERNING AGENTS—A person acting as the agent of a person described in subsection (a) shall not be required to make a supplement to protected health information, except where——

(1) the protected health information is retained by the agent; and

(2) the agent has been asked by such person to fulfill the requirements of this section.

SECTION 111. ESTABLISHMENT OF SAFEGUARDS.

(a) IN GENERAL—A health care provider, health plan, health oversight agency, public health authority, employer, health researcher, law enforcement official, health or life insurer, school, or university, or a person acting as the agent of any such person, shall establish and maintain appropriate administrative, organizational, technical, and physical safeguards and procedures to ensure the confidentiality, security, accuracy, and integrity of protected health information created, received, obtained, maintained, used, transmitted, or disposed of by such person.

(b) FACTORS TO BE CONSIDERED—The policies and safeguards under subsection (a) shall ensure that——

(1) protected health information is used or disclosed only when necessary;

(2) the categories of personnel who will have access to protected health information are identified; and

(3) the feasibility of limiting access to protected health information is considered.

(c) MODEL GUIDELINES—The Secretary, in consultation with the Director of the Office of Health Information Privacy appointed under section 301, after notice and opportunity for public comment, shall develop and disseminate model guidelines for the establishment of safeguards and procedures for use under this section, such as, where appropriate, individual authentication of uses of computer systems, access controls, audit trails, encryption, physical security, protection of remote access points and protection of external electronic communications, periodic security assessments, incident reports, and sanctions. The director shall update and disseminate the guidelines, as appropriate, to take advantage of new technologies.

TITLE II——RESTRICTIONS ON USE AND DISCLOSURE

SECTION 201. GENERAL RULES REGARDING USE AND DISCLOSURE.

(a) PROHIBITION—

(1) GENERAL RULE—A health care provider, health plan, health oversight agency, public health authority, employer, health researcher, law enforcement official, health or life insurer, school, or university may not disclose or use protected health information except as authorized under this Act.

(2) RULE OF CONSTRUCTION—Disclosure of de—identified health information shall not be construed as a disclosure of protected health information.

(b) SCOPE OF DISCLOSURE—

(1) IN GENERAL—A disclosure of protected health information under this title shall be limited to the minimum amount of information necessary to accomplish the purpose for which the disclosure is made.

(2) DETERMINATION—The determination as to what constitutes the minimum disclosure possible for purposes of paragraph (1) shall be made by a health care provider.

(c) USE OR DISCLOSURE FOR PURPOSE ONLY—A recipient of information pursuant to this title may use or disclose such information solely to carry out the purpose for which the information was disclosed.

(d) NO GENERAL REQUIREMENT TO DISCLOSE—Nothing in this title permitting the disclosure of protected health information shall be construed to require such disclosure.

(e) IDENTIFICATION OF DISCLOSED INFORMATION AS PROTECTED HEALTH INFORMATION—Protected health information disclosed pursuant to this title shall be clearly identified as protected health information that is subject to this Act.

(f) DISCLOSURE BY AGENTS—An agent of a person described in subsection (a)(1), who receives protected health information from the person while acting within the scope of the agency, shall be subject to this title to the same extent as the person and for the duration of the period in which the agent holds the information.

(g) CREATION OF DE—IDENTIFIED INFORMATION—Notwithstanding subsection (c), but subject to the other provisions of this section, a person described in subsection (a)(1) may disclose protected health information to an employee or other agent of the person for purposes of creating de—identified information.

(h) UNAUTHORIZED USE OR DISCLOSURE OF THE DECRYPTION KEY—The unauthorized disclosure of a decryption key shall be deemed to be a disclosure of protected health information. The unauthorized use of a decryption key or de—identified health information in order to identify an individual is deemed to be disclosure of protected health information.

(i) NO WAIVER—Except as provided in this Act, an authorization to disclose personally identifiable health information executed by an individual pursuant to section 202 or 203 shall not be construed as a waiver of any rights that the individual has under other Federal or State laws, the rules of evidence, or common law.

(j) DEFINITIONS [omitted]

SECTION 202. AUTHORIZATIONS FOR DISCLOSURE OF PROTECTED HEALTH INFORMATION FOR TREATMENT AND PAYMENT.

(a) REQUIREMENTS RELATING TO EMPLOYERS, HEALTH PLANS, HEALTH OR LIFE INSURERS, UNINSURED INDIVIDUALS, AND PROVIDERS—

(1) IN GENERAL—To satisfy the requirement under section 201(a)(1), an employer, health plan, health or life insurer, or health care provider that seeks to disclose protected health information in connection with treatment or payment shall obtain an authorization that satisfies the requirements of this section. The authorization may be a single authorization.

(2) EMPLOYERS—Every employer offering a health plan to its employees shall, at the time of an employee's enrollment in the health plan, obtain a signed, written authorization that is a legal, informed authorization that satisfies the requirements of subsection (b) concerning the use and disclosure of protected health information for treatment or payment with respect to each individual who is eligible to receive care under the health plan.

(3) HEALTH PLANS, HEALTH OR LIFE INSURERS—Every health plan or health or life insurer offering enrollment to individual or nonemployer groups shall, at the time of enrollment in the plan or insurance, obtain a signed, written authorization that is a legal, informed authorization that satisfies the requirements of subsection

(b) concerning the use and disclosure of protected health information with respect to each individual who is eligible to receive care under the plan or insurance.

(4) UNINSURED—An originating provider providing health care in other than a network plan setting, or providing health care to an uninsured individual, shall obtain a signed, written authorization that satisfies the requirements of subsection (b) to use protected health information in providing health care or arranging for health care from other providers or seeking payment for the provision of health care services.

(5) PROVIDERS—

(A) IN GENERAL—Every health care provider providing health care to an individual who has not given the appropriate authorization under this section shall, at the time of providing such care, obtain a signed, written authorization that is a legal, informed authorization, that satisfies the requirements of subsection (b), concerning the use and disclosure of protected health information with respect to such individual.

(B) RULE OF CONSTRUCTION—Subparagraph (A) shall not be construed to preclude the provision of health care to an individual who has not given appropriate authorization prior to receipt of such care if——

(i) the health care provider involved determines that such care is essential; and

(ii) the individual can reasonably be expected to sign an authorization for such care when appropriate.

(b) REQUIREMENTS FOR INDIVIDUAL AUTHORIZATION—To satisfy the requirements of this subsection, an authorization to disclose protected health information——

(1) shall identify, by general job description or other functional description, persons authorized to disclose the information;

(2) shall describe the nature of the information to be disclosed;

(3) shall identify, by general job description or other functional description, persons to whom the information is to be disclosed, including individuals employed by, or operating within, an entity to which information is authorized to be disclosed;

(4) shall describe the purpose of the disclosures;

(5) shall permit the executing individual to indicate that a particular individual listed on the authorization is not authorized to receive protected health information concerning the individual, except as provided for in subsection (c)(3);

(6) shall provide the means by which an individual may indicate that some of the individual's protected health information should be segregated and to what persons such segregated information may be disclosed;

(7) shall be subject to revocation by the individual and indicate that the authorization is valid until revocation by the individual or until an event or date specified; and

(8)(A) shall be——

(i) in writing, dated, and signed by the individual; or

(ii) in electronic form, dated and authenticated by the individual using an authentication method approved by the Secretary; and

(B) shall not have been revoked under subparagraph (A).

(c) LIMITATION ON AUTHORIZATIONS—

(1) IN GENERAL—Subject to paragraphs (2) and (3), a person described in subsection (a) who seeks an authorization under such subsection may not condition the delivery of treatment or payment for services on the receipt of such an authorization.

(2) RIGHT TO REQUIRE SELF PAYMENT—If an individual has refused to provide an authorization for disclosure of administrative billing information to a person and such authorization is necessary for a health care provider to receive payment for services delivered, the health care provider may require the individual to pay from their own funds for the services.

(3) RIGHT OF HEALTH CARE PROVIDER TO REQUIRE AUTHORIZATION FOR TREATMENT PURPOSES—If a health care provider that is seeking an authorization for disclosure of an individual's protected health information believes that the disclosure of such information is necessary so as not to endanger the health or treatment of the individual, the health care provider may condition the provision of services upon the execution of the authorization by the individual.

(d) MODEL AUTHORIZATIONS—The Secretary, in consultation with the Director of the Office of Health Information Privacy, after notice and opportunity for public comment, shall develop and disseminate model written authorizations of the type described in this section and model statements of the limitations on authorizations. Any authorization obtained on a model authorization form under section 202 developed by the Secretary pursuant to the preceding sentence shall be deemed to satisfy the requirements of this section.

(e) SEGREGATION OF FILES—A person described in subsection (a)(1) shall comply, to the maximum extent practicable, with the request of an individual who is the subject of protected health information——

(1) to segregate any type or amount of protected health information, other than administrative billing information, held by the entity; and

(2) to limit the use or disclosure of the segregated health information within the entity to those persons specifically designated by the subject of the protected health information.

(f) REVOCATION OF AUTHORIZATION—

(1) IN GENERAL—An individual may in writing revoke or amend an authorization under this section at any time, unless the disclosure that is the subject of the authorization is required to effectuate payment for health care that has been provided to the individual.

(2) HEALTH PLANS—With respect to a health plan, the authorization of an individual is deemed to be revoked at the time of the cancellation or non—renewal of enrollment in the health plan, except as may be necessary to complete plan administration and payment requirements related to the individual's period of enrollment.

(3) ACTIONS—An individual may not maintain an action against a person for disclosure of personally identifiable health information——

(A) if the disclosure was made based on a good faith reliance on the individual's authorization under this section at the time disclosure was made;

(B) in a case in which the authorization is revoked, if the disclosing person had no actual or constructive notice of the revocation; or

(C) if the disclosure was for the purpose of protecting another individual from imminent physical harm, and is authorized under section 204.

(g) RECORD OF INDIVIDUAL'S AUTHORIZATIONS AND REVOCATIONS—Each person collecting or storing personally identifiable health information shall maintain a record for a period of 7 years of each authorization of an individual and any revocation thereof, and such record shall become part of the personally identifiable health information concerning such individual.

(h) RULE OF CONSTRUCTION—Authorizations for the disclosure of protected health information for treatment or payment shall not authorize the disclosure of such information by an individual with the intent to sell, transfer, or use protected health information for commercial advantage other than the revenues directly derived from the provision of health care to that individual. For such disclosures, a separate authorization that satisfies the requirements of section 203 is required.

SECTION 203. AUTHORIZATIONS FOR DISCLOSURE OF PROTECTED HEALTH INFORMATION OTHER THAN FOR TREATMENT OR PAYMENT.

(a) IN GENERAL—To satisfy the requirement under section 201(a)(1), a health care provider, health plan, health oversight agency, public health authority, employer, health researcher, law enforcement official, health or life insurer, school, or university that seeks to disclose protected health information for a purpose other than treatment or payment may obtain an authorization that satisfies the requirements of subsections (b) and (g) of section 202. Such an authorization under this section shall be separate from an authorization provided under section 202.

(b) LIMITATION ON AUTHORIZATIONS—

(1) IN GENERAL—A person subject to section 202 may not condition the delivery of treatment, or payment for services, on the receipt of an authorization described in this section.

(2) REQUIREMENT FOR SEPARATE AUTHORIZATION—A person subject to section 202 may not disclose protected health information to any employees or agents who are responsible for making employment, work assignment, or other personnel decisions with respect to the subject of the information without a separate authorization permitting such a disclosure.

(c) MODEL AUTHORIZATIONS—The Secretary, in consultation with the Director of the Office of Health Information Privacy, after notice and opportunity for public comment, shall develop and disseminate model written authorizations of the type described in subsection (a). Any authorization obtained on a model authorization form under this section developed by the Secretary shall be deemed to meet the authorization requirements of this section.

(d) REQUIREMENT TO RELEASE PROTECTED HEALTH INFORMATION TO CORONERS AND MEDICAL EXAMINERS—

(1) IN GENERAL—When a Coroner or Medical Examiner or their duly appointed deputies seek protected health information for the purpose of inquiry into and determination of, the cause, manner, and circumstances of an individual's death, the health care provider, health plan, health oversight agency, public health authority, employer, health researcher, law enforcement officer, health or life insurer, school or university involved shall provide that individual's protected health information to the Coroner or Medical Examiner or to the duly appointed deputies without undue delay.

(2) PRODUCTION OF ADDITIONAL INFORMATION—If a Coroner or Medical Examiner or their duly appointed deputies receives health information from an entity referred to in paragraph (1), such health information shall remain as protected health information unless the health information is attached to or otherwise made a part of a Coroner's or Medical Examiner's official report, in which case it shall no longer be protected.

(3) EXEMPTION—Health information attached to or otherwise made a part of a Coroner's or Medical Examiner's official report, shall be exempt from the provisions of this Act except as provided for in this subsection.

(4) REIMBURSEMENT—A Coroner or Medical Examiner may require a person to reimburse their Office for the reasonable costs associated with such inspection or copying.

(e) REVOCATION OR AMENDMENT OF AUTHORIZATION—An individual may, in writing, revoke or amend an authorization under this section at any time.

(f) ACTIONS—An individual may not maintain an action against a person for disclosure of protected health information——

(1) if the disclosure was made based on a good faith reliance on the individual's authorization under this section at the time disclosure was made;

(2) in a case in which the authorization is revoked, if the disclosing person had no actual or constructive notice of the revocation; or

(3) if the disclosure was for the purpose of protecting another individual from imminent physical harm, and is authorized under section 204.

SECTION 204. EMERGENCY CIRCUMSTANCES.

(a) GENERAL RULE—In the event of a threat of imminent physical or mental harm to the subject of protected health information, any person may, in order to allay or remedy such threat, disclose protected health information about such subject to a health care practitioner, health care facility, law enforcement authority, or emergency medical personnel.

(b) HARM TO OTHERS—Any person may disclose protected health information about the subject of the information where——

(1) such subject has made an identifiable threat of serious injury or death with respect to an identifiable individual or group of individuals;

(2) the subject has the ability to carry out such threat; and

(3) the release of such information is necessary to prevent or significantly reduce the possibility of such threat being carried out.

SECTION 205. PUBLIC HEALTH.

(a) IN GENERAL—A health care provider, health plan, public health authority, employer, health or life insurer, law enforcement official, school, or university may disclose protected health information to a public health authority or other person authorized by public health law when receipt of such information by the authority or other person——

(1) relates directly to a specified public health purpose;

(2) is reasonably likely to achieve such purpose; and

(3) is intended for a purpose that cannot be achieved through the receipt or use of de—identified health information.

(b) PUBLIC HEALTH PURPOSE DEFINED—For purposes of subsection (a), the term `public health purpose' means a population—based activity or individual effort, authorized by law, aimed at the prevention of injury, disease, or premature mortality, or the promotion of health, in a community, including——

(1) assessing the health needs and status of the community through public health surveillance and epidemiological research;

(2) developing public health policy;

(3) responding to public health needs and emergencies; and

(4) any other activities or efforts authorized by law.

SECTION 206. PROTECTION AND ADVOCACY AGENCIES.

Any person who creates protected health information or receives protected health information under this title may disclose that information to a protection and advocacy agency established under part C of title I of the Developmental Disabilities Assistance and Bill of Rights Act (42 U.S.C. 6041 et seq.) or under the Protection and Advocacy for Mentally Ill Individuals Act of 1986 (42 U.S.C. 10801 et seq.) when such agency can establish that there is probable cause to believe that an individual who is the subject of the protected health information is vulnerable to abuse and neglect by an entity providing health or social services to the individual.

SECTION 207. OVERSIGHT.

(a) IN GENERAL—A health care provider, health plan, employer, law enforcement official, health or life insurer, public health authority, health researcher, school or university may disclose protected health information to a health oversight agency to enable the agency to perform a health oversight function authorized by law, if——

(1) the purpose for which the disclosure is to be made cannot reasonably be accomplished without protected health information;

(2) the purpose for which the disclosure is to be made is of sufficient importance to warrant the effect on, or the risk to, the privacy of the individuals that additional exposure of the information might bring; and

(3) there is a reasonable probability that the purpose of the disclosure will be accomplished.

(b) USE AND MAINTENANCE OF PROTECTED HEALTH INFORMATION—A health oversight agency that receives protected health information under this section——

(1) shall rely upon a method to scramble or otherwise safeguard, to the maximum extent practicable, the identity of the subject of the protected health information in all work papers and all documents summarizing the health oversight activity;

(2) shall maintain in its records only such information about an individual as is relevant and necessary to accomplish the purpose for which the protected health information was obtained;

(3) shall maintain such information securely and limit access to such information to those persons with a legitimate need for access to carry out the purpose for which the records were obtained; and

(4) shall remove or destroy the information that allows subjects of protected health information to be identified at the earliest time at which removal or destruction can be accomplished, consistent with the purpose of the health oversight activity.

(c) USE OF PROTECTED HEALTH INFORMATION IN JUDICIAL PROCEEDINGS—

(1) IN GENERAL—The disclosure and use of protected health information in any judicial, administrative, court, or other public, proceeding or investigation relating to a health oversight activity shall be undertaken in such a manner as to preserve the confidentiality and privacy of individuals who are the subject of the information, unless disclosure is required by the nature of the proceedings.

(2) LIMITING DISCLOSURE—Whenever disclosure of the identity of the subject of protected health information is required by the nature of the proceedings, or it is impracticable to redact the identity of such individual, the agency shall request that the presiding judicial or administrative officer enter an order limiting the disclosure of the identity of the subject to the extent possible, including the redacting of the protected health information from publicly disclosed or filed pleadings or records.

(d) AUTHORIZATION BY A SUPERVISOR—For purposes of this section, the individual with authority to authorize the oversight function involved shall provide to the disclosing person described in subsection (a) a statement that the protected health information is being sought for a legally authorized oversight function.

(e) USE IN ACTION AGAINST INDIVIDUALS—Protected health information about an individual that is disclosed under this section may not be used in, or disclosed to any person for use in, an administrative, civil, or criminal action or investigation directed against the individual, unless the action or investigation arises out of and is directly related to——

(1) the receipt of health care or payment for health care;

(2) a fraudulent claim related to health; or

(3) oversight of a public health authority or a health researcher.

SECTION 208. DISCLOSURE FOR LAW ENFORCEMENT PURPOSES.

(a) LAW ENFORCEMENT ACCESS TO PROTECTED HEALTH INFORMATION—A health care provider, health researcher, health plan, health oversight agency, employer, health or life insurer, school, university, a person acting as the agent of any such person, or a person who receives protected health information pursuant to section 204, may disclose protected health information to an investigative or law enforcement officer pursuant to a warrant issued under the Federal Rules of Criminal Procedure, an equivalent State warrant, a grand jury subpoena, or a court order under limitations set forth in subsection (b).

(b) REQUIREMENTS FOR COURT ORDERS FOR ACCESS TO PROTECTED HEALTH INFORMATION—A court order for the disclosure of protected health information under subsection (a) may be issued by any court that is a court of competent jurisdiction and shall issue only if the investigative or law enforcement officer submits a written application upon oath or equivalent affirmation demonstrating that there is probable cause to believe that——

(1) the protected health information sought is relevant and material to an ongoing criminal investigation, except in the case of a State government authority, such a court order shall not issue if prohibited by the law of such State;

(2) the investigative or evidentiary needs of the investigative or law enforcement officer cannot reasonably be satisfied by de—identified health information or by any other information; and

(3) the law enforcement need for the information outweighs the privacy interest of the individual to whom the information pertains.

(c) MOTIONS TO QUASH OR MODIFY—A court issuing an order pursuant to this section, on a motion made promptly by the health care provider, health researcher, health plan, health oversight agency, employer, health or life insurer, school, university, a person acting as the agent of any such person, or a person who receives protected health information pursuant to section 204, may quash or modify such order if the court finds that information or records requested are unreasonably voluminous or if compliance with such order otherwise would cause an unreasonable burden on such persons.

(d) NOTICE—

(1) IN GENERAL—Except as provided in paragraph (2), no order for the disclosure of protected health information about an individual may be issued by a court under this section unless prior notice of the application for the order has been served on the individual and the individual has been afforded an opportunity to oppose the issuance of the order.

(2) NOTICE NOT REQUIRED—An order for the disclosure of protected health information about an individual may be issued without prior notice to the individual if the court finds that notice would be impractical because——

(A) the name and address of the individual are unknown; or

(B) notice would risk destruction or unavailability of the evidence.

(e) CONDITIONS—Upon the granting of an order for disclosure of protected health information under this section, the court shall impose appropriate safeguards to ensure the confidentiality of such information and to protect against unauthorized or improper use or disclosure.

(f) LIMITATION ON USE AND DISCLOSURE FOR OTHER LAW ENFORCEMENT INQUIRIES—Protected health information about an individual that is disclosed under this section may not be used in, or disclosed to any person for use in, any administrative, civil, or criminal action or investigation directed against the individual, unless the action or investigation arises out of, or is directly related to, the law enforcement inquiry for which the information was obtained.

(g) DESTRUCTION OR RETURN OF INFORMATION—When the matter or need for which protected health information was disclosed to an investigative or law enforcement officer or grand jury has concluded, including any derivative matters arising from such matter or need, the law enforcement agency or grand jury shall either destroy the protected health information, or return it to the person from whom it was obtained.

(h) REDACTIONS—To the extent practicable, and consistent with the requirements of due process, a law enforcement agency shall redact personally identifying information from protected health information prior to the public disclosure of such protected information in a judicial or administrative proceeding.

(i) EXCEPTION—This section shall not be construed to limit or restrict the ability of law enforcement authorities to gain information while in hot pursuit of a suspect or if other exigent circumstances exist.

SECTION 209. NEXT OF KIN AND DIRECTORY INFORMATION.

(a) NEXT OF KIN—A health care provider, or a person who receives protected health information under section 204, may disclose protected health information about health care services provided to an individual to the individual's next of kin, or to another person whom the individual has identified, if at the time of the treatment of the individual——

(1) the individual——

(A) has been notified of the individual's right to object to such disclosure and the individual has not objected to the disclosure; or

(B) is in a physical or mental condition such that the individual is not capable of objecting, and there are no prior indications that the individual would object; and

(2) the information disclosed relates to health care services currently being provided to that individual.

(b) DIRECTORY INFORMATION—

(1) DISCLOSURE—

(A) IN GENERAL—Except as provided in paragraph (2), with respect to an individual who is admitted as an inpatient to a health care facility, a person described in subsection (a) may disclose information described in subparagraph (B) about the individual to any person if, at the time of the admission, the individual——

(i) has been notified of the individual's right to object and has not objected to the disclosure; or

(ii) is in a physical or mental condition such that the individual is not capable of objecting and there are no prior indications that the individual would object.

(B) INFORMATION—Information described in this subparagraph is information that consists only of 1 or more of the following items:

(i) The name of the individual who is the subject of the information.

(ii) The general health status of the individual, described as critical, poor, fair, stable, or satisfactory or in terms denoting similar conditions.

(iii) The location of the individual within the health care facility to which the individual is admitted.

(2) EXCEPTION—Paragraph (1)(B)(iii) shall not apply if disclosure of the location of the individual would reveal specific information about the physical or mental condition of the individual, unless the individual expressly authorizes such disclosure.

(c) DIRECTORY OR NEXT—OF—KIN INFORMATION—A disclosure may not be made under this section if the disclosing person described in subsection (a) has reason to believe that the disclosure of directory or next—of—kin information could lead to the physical or mental harm of the individual, unless the individual expressly authorizes such disclosure.

SECTION 210. HEALTH RESEARCH [OMITTED]

SECTION 211. JUDICIAL AND ADMINISTRATIVE PURPOSES.

(a) IN GENERAL—A health care provider, health plan, health oversight agency, employer, insurer, health or life insurer, school or university, a person acting as the agent of any such person, or a person who receives protected health information under section 204, may disclose protected health information——

(1) pursuant to the standards and procedures established in the Federal Rules of Civil Procedure or comparable rules of other courts or administrative agencies, in connection with litigation or proceedings to which an individual who is the subject of the information is a party and in which the individual has placed his or her physical or mental condition at issue;

(2) to a court, and to others ordered by the court, if in response to a court order issued by a court of competent jurisdiction in accordance with subsections (b) and (c); or

(3) if necessary to present to a court an application regarding the provision of treatment of an individual or the appointment of a guardian.

(b) COURT ORDERS FOR ACCESS TO PROTECTED HEALTH INFORMATION—A court order for the disclosure of protected health information under subsection (a) may be issued only if the person seeking disclosure submits a written application upon oath or equivalent affirmation demonstrating by clear and convincing evidence that——

(1) the protected health information sought is necessary for the adjudication of a material fact in dispute in a civil proceeding;

(2) the adjudicative need cannot be reasonably satisfied by de—identified health information or by any other information; and

(3) the need for the information outweighs the privacy interest of the individual to whom the information pertains.

(c) NOTICE—

(1) IN GENERAL—Except as provided in paragraph (2), no order for the disclosure of protected health information about an individual may be issued by a court unless notice of the application for the order has been served on the individual and the individual has been afforded an opportunity to oppose the issuance of the order.

(2) NOTICE NOT REQUIRED—An order for the disclosure of protected health information about an individual may be issued without notice to the individual if the court finds, by clear and convincing evidence, that notice would be impractical because——

(A) the name and address of the individual are unknown; or

(B) notice would risk destruction or unavailability of the evidence.

(d) OBLIGATIONS OF RECIPIENT—A person seeking protected health information pursuant to subsection (a)(1)——

(1) shall notify the individual or the individual's attorney of the request for the information;

(2) shall provide the health care provider, health plan, health oversight agency, employer, insurer, health or life insurer, school or university, agent, or other person involved with a signed document attesting——

(A) that the individual has placed his or her physical or mental condition at issue in litigation or proceedings in which the individual is a party; and

(B) the date on which the individual or the individual's attorney was notified under paragraph (1); and

(3) shall not accept any requested protected health information from the health care provider, health plan, health oversight agency, employer, insurer, health or life insurer, school or university, agent, or person until the termination of the 10—day period beginning on the date notice was given under paragraph (1).

SECTION 212. INDIVIDUAL REPRESENTATIVES.

(a) IN GENERAL—Except as provided in subsections (b) and (c), a person who is authorized by law (based on grounds other than an individual's status as a minor), or by an instrument recognized under law, to act as an agent, attorney, proxy, or other legal representative of a individual, may, to the extent so authorized, exercise and discharge the rights of the individual under this Act.

(b) HEALTH CARE POWER OF ATTORNEY—A person who is authorized by law (based on grounds other than being a minor), or by an instrument recognized under law, to make decisions about the provision of health care to an individual who is incapacitated, may exercise and discharge the rights of the individual under this Act to the extent necessary to effectuate the terms or purposes of the grant of authority.

(c) NO COURT DECLARATION—If a physician or other health care provider determines that an individual, who has not been declared to be legally incompetent, suffers from a medical condition that prevents the individual from acting knowingly or effectively on the individual's own behalf, the right of the individual to authorize disclosure under this Act may be exercised and discharged in the best interest of the individual by——

(1) a person described in subsection (b) with respect to the individual;

(2) a person described in subsection (a) with respect to the individual, but only if a person described in paragraph (1) cannot be contacted after a reasonable effort;

(3) the next of kin of the individual, but only if a person described in paragraph (1) or (2) cannot be contacted after a reasonable effort; or

(4) the health care provider, but only if a person described in paragraph (1), (2), or (3) cannot be contacted after a reasonable effort.

(d) RIGHTS OF MINORS—

(1) INDIVIDUALS WHO ARE 18 OR LEGALLY CAPABLE—In the case of an individual——

(A) who is 18 years of age or older, all rights of the individual under this Act shall be exercised by the individual; or

(B) who, acting alone, can obtain a type of health care without violating any applicable law, and who has sought such care, the individual shall exercise all rights of an individual under this Act with respect to protected health information relating to such health care.

(2) INDIVIDUALS UNDER 18—Except as provided in paragraph (1)(B), in the case of an individual who is——

(A) under 14 years of age, all of the individual's rights under this Act shall be exercised through the parent or legal guardian; or

(B) 14 through 17 years of age, the rights of inspection and supplementation, and the right to authorize use and disclosure of protected health information of the individual shall be exercised by the individual, or by the parent or legal guardian of the individual.

(e) DECEASED INDIVIDUALS—

(1) APPLICATION OF ACT—The provisions of this Act shall continue to apply to protected health information concerning a deceased individual.

(2) EXERCISE OF RIGHTS ON BEHALF OF A DECEASED INDIVIDUAL—A person who is authorized by law or by an instrument recognized under law, to act as an executor of the estate of a deceased individual, or otherwise to exercise the rights of the deceased individual, may, to the extent so authorized, exercise and discharge the rights of such deceased individual under this Act. If no such designee has been authorized, the rights of the deceased individual may be exercised as provided for in subsection (c).

(3) IDENTIFICATION OF DECEASED INDIVIDUAL—A person described in section 209(a) may disclose protected health information if such disclosure is necessary to assist in the identification of a deceased individual.

SECTION 213. PROHIBITION AGAINST RETALIATION.

A health care provider, health researcher, health plan, health oversight agency, employer, health or life insurer, school or university, person acting as an agent of any such person, or person who receives protected health information under section 204 may not adversely affect another person, directly or indirectly, because such person has exercised a right under this Act, disclosed information relating to a possible violation of this Act, or associated with, or assisted, a person in the exercise of a right under this Act.

TITLE III——OFFICE OF HEALTH INFORMATION PRIVACY OF THE DEPARTMENT OF HEALTH AND HUMAN SERVICES

SUBTITLE A——DESIGNATION [OMITTED]

SUBTITLE B——ENFORCEMENT

CHAPTER 1——CRIMINAL PROVISIONS

SECTION 311. WRONGFUL DISCLOSURE OF PROTECTED HEALTH INFORMATION.

(a) IN GENERAL—Part I of title 18, United States Code, is amended by adding at the end the following:

`CHAPTER 124——WRONGFUL DISCLOSURE OF PROTECTED HEALTH INFORMATION

`Sec. 2801. Wrongful disclosure of protected health information

`(a) OFFENSE—The penalties described in subsection (b) shall apply to a person that knowingly and intentionally——

`(1) obtains or attempts to obtain protected health information relating to an individual in violation of title II of the Medical Information Privacy and Security Act; or

`(2) discloses or attempts to disclose protected health information to another person in violation of title II of the Medical Information Privacy and Security Act.

`(b) PENALTIES—A person described in subsection (a) shall——

`(1) be fined not more than $50,000, imprisoned not more than 1 year, or both;

`(2) if the offense is committed under false pretenses, be fined not more than $250,000, imprisoned not more than 5 years, or any combination of such penalties; or

`(3) if the offense is committed with the intent to sell, transfer, or use protected health information for commercial advantage, personal gain, or malicious harm, be fined not more than $500,000, imprisoned not more than 10 years, excluded from participation in any Federally funded health care programs, or any combination of such penalties.

`(c) SUBSEQUENT OFFENSES—In the case of a person described in subsection (a), the maximum penalties described in subsection (b) shall be doubled for every subsequent conviction for an offense arising out of a violation or violations related to a set of circumstances that are different from those involved in the previous violation or set of related violations described in such subsection (a).'.

(b) CLERICAL AMENDMENT—The table of chapters for part I of title 18, United States Code, is amended by inserting after the item relating to chapter 123 the following new item:

2801'.

SECTION 312. DEBARMENT FOR CRIMES.

(a) PURPOSE—The purpose of this section is to promote the prevention and deterrence of instances of intentional criminal actions which violate criminal laws which are designed to protect the privacy of protected health information in a manner consistent with this Act.

(b) DEBARMENT—Not later than 270 days after the date of enactment of this Act, the Attorney General, in consultation with the Secretary, shall promulgate regulations and establish procedures to permit the debarment of health care providers, health researchers, health or life insurers, employers, or schools or universities from receiving benefits under any Federal health programs or other Federal procurement program if the managers or officers of such persons are found guilty of violating section 2801 of title 18, United States Code, have civil penalties imposed against such officers or managers under section 321 in connection with the illegal disclosure of protected health information, or are found guilty of making a false statement or obstructing justice related to attempting to conceal or concealing such illegal disclosure. Such regulations shall take into account the need for continuity of medical care and may provide for a delay of any debarment imposed under this section to take into account the medical needs of patients.

(c) CONSULTATION—Before publishing a proposed rule to implement subsection (b), the Attorney General shall consult with State law enforcement officials, health care providers, patient privacy rights' advocates, and other appropriate persons, to gain additional information regarding the debarment of entities under subsection (b) and the best methods to ensure the continuity of medical care.

(d) REPORT—The Attorney General shall annually prepare and submit to the Committee on the Judiciary of the House of Representatives and the Committee on the Judiciary of the Senate a report concerning the activities and debarment actions taken by the Attorney General under this section.

(e) ASSISTANCE TO PREVENT CRIMINAL VIOLATIONS—The Attorney General, in cooperation with any other appropriate individual, organization, or agency, may provide advice, training, technical assistance, and guidance regarding ways to reduce the incidence of improper disclosure of protected health information.

(f) RELATIONSHIP TO OTHER AUTHORITIES—A debarment imposed under this section shall not reduce or diminish the authority of a Federal, State, or local governmental agency or court to penalize, imprison, fine, suspend, debar, or take other adverse action against a person, in a civil, criminal, or administrative proceeding.

CHAPTER 2——CIVIL SANCTIONS

SECTION 321. CIVIL PENALTY.

(a) VIOLATION—A health care provider, health researcher, health plan, health oversight agency, public health agency, law enforcement agency, employer, health or life insurer, school, or university, or a person acting as the agent of any such person, who the Secretary, in consultation with the Attorney General, determines has substantially and materially failed to comply with this Act shall be subject, in addition to any other penalties that may be prescribed by law——

(1) in a case in which the violation relates to title I, to a civil penalty of not more than $500 for each such violation, but not to exceed $5000 in the aggregate for multiple violations;

(2) in a case in which the violation relates to title II, to a civil penalty of not more than $10,000 for each such violation, but not to exceed $50,000 in the aggregate for multiple violations; or

(3) in a case in which the Secretary finds that such violations have occurred with such frequency as to constitute a general business practice, to a civil penalty of not more than $100,000.

(b) PROCEDURES FOR IMPOSITION OF PENALTIES—Section 1128A of the Social Security Act (42 U.S.C. 1320a—7a), other than subsections (a) and (b) and the second sentence of subsection (f) of that section, shall apply to the imposition of a civil, monetary, or exclusionary penalty under this section in the same manner as such provisions apply with respect to the imposition of a penalty under section 1128A of such Act.

SECTION 322. PROCEDURES FOR IMPOSITION OF PENALTIES [OMITTED]

SECTION 323. CIVIL ACTION BY INDIVIDUALS.

(a) IN GENERAL—Any individual whose rights under this Act have been knowingly or negligently violated may bring a civil action to recover——

(1) such preliminary and equitable relief as the court determines to be appropriate; and

(2) the greater of compensatory damages or liquidated damages of $5,000.

(b) PUNITIVE DAMAGES—In any action brought under this section in which the individual has prevailed because of a knowing violation of a provision of this Act, the court may, in addition to any relief awarded under subsection (a), award such punitive damages as may be warranted.

(c) ATTORNEY'S FEES—In the case of a civil action brought under subsection (a) in which the individual has substantially prevailed, the court may assess against the respondent a reasonable attorney's fee and other litigation costs and expenses (including expert fees) reasonably incurred.

(d) LIMITATION—No action may be commenced under this section more than 3 years after the date on which the violation was or should reasonably have been discovered.

(e) AGENCY—A principal is jointly and severally liable with the principal's agent for damages under this section for the actions of the principal's agent acting within the scope of the agency.

(f) ADDITIONAL REMEDIES—The equitable relief or damages that may be available under this section shall be in additional to any other lawful remedy or award available.

TITLE IV——MISCELLANEOUS [OMITTED]

APPENDIX 13: SAMPLE LETTER REQUESTING INFORMATION CONCERNING HEALTH PLAN COVERAGE TERMS

[Date] ______________________

[Health Plan] ______________________

[address] ____

RE: Request for Information—[Name]-[Social Security No.]

Dear Sir/Madam:

I am writing to request information concerning the terms of my health plan coverage. On [date], I contacted your office by telephone and requested this information, but I have not yet received a response.

My Summary Plan Description states that I am entitled to the material I have requested. In addition, according to [relevant state law], health plans are required to provide me with the following information:

> [Describe the information requested, e.g. the plan contract; the plan's formulary (list of approved drugs) etc.]

Please provide me with the requested information as soon as possible. Thank you for your attention to this serious matter.

Sincerely,

[Name] ______________________

Enclosures: [list and attach all relevant documentation, e.g., copy of Summary Plan Description which sets forth rights to requested information]

APPENDIX 14: SAMPLE LETTER REQUESTING COVERAGE FOR NON-FORMULARY PRESCRIPTION DRUG

[Date] ______________________

[Health Plan] ______________________

[address] ____

RE: Request for Coverage of Non-Formulary Prescription Drug

[Name]-[Social Security No.]______________________

Dear Sir/Madam:

I am writing to request that XYZ Insurance Company cover the cost of my prescription for [name of medication]. XYZ has denied coverage for [name of medication] because it is not included on the health plan's formulary. However, [name of medication] is medically necessary for my condition, is recommended and prescribed by my doctor, and there are no alternative drugs on the formulary that are suitable for treating my condition.

In addition, I have been taking [name of medication] for [time period, e.g. 6 months], and a change of medication could have detrimental effects on my health. Thus, the plan should cover the cost of [name of medication] in my case.

Please be advised that failure to provide [name of medication] as treatment for my condition involves an imminent and serious threat to my health. I am therefore requesting an expedited review of my request for coverage of this medication. Please provide me with a decision as soon as possible, and no later than [time specified in Summary Plan Description] from the date of this request.

I am attaching documentation of my medical condition and information supporting the medical necessity of [name of medication] to assist you with your decision.

Thank you for your attention to this serious matter.

Sincerely,

[Name]______________________

Enclosures: [list and attach all relevant documentation, e.g., letter from health care provider; relevant medical documentation; copy of Summary Plan Description section concerning the plan's formulary, etc.]

APPENDIX 15: SAMPLE GRIEVANCE LETTER TO STATE REGULATORY AGENCY

[Date] ______________________

[State Regulatory Agency] ______________________

[address] ____

RE: Grievance against [Health Plan]

[Name]-[Social Security No.] ________________________________

Dear Sir/Madam:

On [date] I filed a grievance with XYZ Insurance Company. I am requesting assistance from the [state regulatory agency] in resolving my difficulties with my plan because I do not agree with their decision in the following matter:

[Describe underlying circumstances]

I have enclosed copies of all of the documentation concerning this dispute with XYZ Insurance Company.

Thank you for your attention to this serious matter.

Sincerely,

[Name] ______________________

Enclosures: [list and attach all relevant documentation]

APPENDIX 16: SAMPLE APPEAL LETTER FOR SERVICES DENIED AS NOT MEDICALLY NECESSARY

[Date] ______________________

[Health Plan] ______________________

[address]____

RE: Appeal for [Name]-[Social Security No.]________________

Dear Sir/Madam:

I am writing to appeal XYZ Insurance Company's decision to deny authorization for [describe the service/procedure/treatment] under my plan. XYZ has denied coverage for this [service/procedure/treatment], as not medically necessary. I believe this [service/procedure/treatment] is medically necessary to [treat/diagnose] my medical condition and is covered by my health plan. I request that XYZ Insurance Company reconsider its denial for coverage of this [service/procedure/treatment] in my case.

Please be advised that failure to provide immediate treatment for my condition involves an imminent and serious threat to my health. I am therefore requesting an expedited review of my request for coverage of this medication. Please provide me with a decision as soon as possible, and no later than [time specified in Summary Plan Description] from the date of this request.

Please be further advised that the Summary Plan Description's definition of medical necessity [Page #] is as follows:

> [insert plan definition of medical necessity from your Summary Plan Description]

As explained below, this requested [service/procedure/treatment], for addressing my condition, falls within this definition. I note that the plan excludes treatments and procedures listed on [Page #] of my Summary Plan Description. The [service/procedure/treatment] sought is not listed as an exclusion or limitation under my health plan coverage.

Further, this [service/procedure/treatment] is recommended for my condition by [name of health care provider], as set forth in the attached letter. Further, the [service/procedure/treatment] is within the standards of good clinical practice.

According to my health care provider, I have [condition], which [describe limitations, symptoms, etc.] I have previously received [types of other treatments you have tried, or diagnostic tests you have undergone, if any] to treat this condition. However, my health problems have not been resolved. Without the prescribed treatment, I will continue to suffer from this condition. If left untreated, my condition may require even more complex and costly treatment in the future.

I am attaching documentation of my medical condition and information supporting the medical necessity of this [service/procedure/treatment] to assist you with your decision.

Thank you for your attention to this serious matter.

Sincerely,

[Name] ____

Enclosures: [list and attach all relevant documentation, e.g., letter from health care provider; relevant medical documentation; relevant pages of Summary Plan Description, etc.]

APPENDIX 17: SAMPLE APPEAL LETTER FOR SERVICES DENIED AS NOT A COVERED BENEFIT

[Date] ______________________

[Health Plan] ______________________

[address] ______________________________________

RE: Appeal for [Name]-[Social Security No.] ______________

Dear Sir/Madam:

I am writing to appeal XYZ Insurance Company's decision to deny authorization for [describe service/procedure/treatment] under my plan. XYZ has denied coverage for this [service/procedure/treatment], as not a covered benefit under my plan. I believe [service/procedure/treatment] is medically necessary to treat my medical condition and is a covered plan benefit. XYZ should approve [service/procedure/treatment] in my case.

Please be advised that failure to provide immediate treatment for my condition involves an imminent and serious threat to my health. I am therefore requesting an expedited review of my request for coverage of this medication. Please provide me with a decision as soon as possible, and no later than [time specified in Summary Plan Description] from the date of this request.

XYZ covers medically necessary services that are not specifically excluded, in addition to services specifically included under the plan terms. My health plan specifically includes coverage for [service/procedure/treatment] as set forth on [Page #] of the Summary Plan Description.

[state specific reference]

Further, the plan excludes treatments and procedures listed on [Page #] of my Summary Plan Description and the treatment sought is not listed as an exclusion or limitation under my health plan coverage.

Further, this [service/procedure/treatment] is recommended for my condition by [name of health care provider], as set forth in the attached letter. Further, the [service/procedure/treatment] is within the standards of good clinical practice.

According to my health care provider, I have [condition], which [describe limitations, symptoms, etc.] I have previously received [types of other treatments you have tried, or diagnostic tests you have undergone, if any] to treat this condition. However, my health problems have not been resolved. Without the prescribed treatment, I will continue to suffer from this condition. If left untreated, my condition may require even more complex and costly treatment in the future.

I am attaching documentation of my medical condition and information supporting the medical necessity of this [service/procedure/treatment] to assist you with your decision.

Thank you for your attention to this serious matter.

Sincerely,

[Name] ____

Enclosures: [list and attach all relevant documentation, e.g., letter from health care provider; relevant medical documentation; relevant pages of Summary Plan Description, etc.]

APPENDIX 18: SAMPLE QUALITY OF CARE COMPLAINT LETTER

[Date] ______________________________

[Health Plan] ______________________________

[address]____

RE: Complaint Against [Name of Health Care Provider]

[Name]-[Social Security No.] _____________________________________

Dear Sir/Madam:

I am writing to express my dissatisfaction with services I received from [name of provider] on [date]. I am unhappy with the services provided by [name of provider] for the following reasons:

> [Provide all details of the complaint including facts surrounding treatment; what should have been done; damages, if any; names of witnesses, etc.]

I am requesting you to investigate this matter and take appropriate action. Please notify me in writing of the results of your investigation.

Thank you for your attention to this serious matter.

Sincerely,

[Name] ____

Enclosures: [list and attach all relevant documentation]

APPENDIX 19: SAMPLE LETTER TO HEALTH INSURANCE PLAN CONCERNING BILLING PROBLEM

[Date] ______________________________

[Health Plan] ______________________________

[address] ____

RE: Billing Inquiry—[Name]-[Social Security No.]____________

Dear Sir/Madam:

I am writing to request that XYZ Insurance Company cover a bill I received for [provide details]. The service was provided on [date] by [name of health care provider]. The bill I received is for [dollar amount] and must be paid by [due date].

I believe this bill should is covered under my health plan. I called XYZ on [date], and spoke with [name of customer service representative] concerning the bill, but the problem has not yet been resolved. Attached is documentation which supports my position that this bill represents a covered service.

I would appreciate if you would consider this matter and provide me with your written decision.

Thank you for your attention to this serious matter.

Sincerely,

[Name] ____

Enclosures: [list and attach all relevant documentation] Please respond in writing and let me know what actions you will take regarding this request. Thank you for your prompt attention to this matter.

Sincerely,

[Your name] ____

APPENDIX 20: MEDICARE PATIENT'S STATEMENT OF RIGHTS

As a Medicare beneficiary, you have certain guaranteed rights. These rights protect you when you get health care; they assure you access to needed health care services; and they protect you against unethical practices. You have these Medicare rights whether you are in the Original Medicare Plan or another Medicare health plan. Your rights include:

1. The right to protection from discrimination in marketing and enrollment practices.

2. The right to information about what is covered and how much you have to pay.

3. The right to information about all treatment options available to you. You have the right to information about all your health care treatment options from your health care provider. Medicare forbids its health plans from making any rules that would stop a doctor from telling you everything you need to know about your health care, including treatment options. If you think your Medicare health plan may have kept your health care provider from telling you everything you need to know about your health care treatment options, you have a right to appeal.

4. The right to receive emergency care. If you have severe pain, an injury, sudden illness, or a suddenly worsening illness that you believe may cause your health serious danger without immediate care, you have the right to receive emergency care. You never need prior approval for emergency care, and you may receive emergency care anywhere in the United States.

5. The right to appeal decisions to deny or limit payment for medical care. If you are in the Original Medicare Plan, you have the right to appeal a denial of payment for a service you have been provided. Likewise, if you are enrolled in one of the other Medicare health plans, you have the right to appeal the plan's denial for a service to

be provided. As a Medicare beneficiary, you always have the right to appeal these decisions.

6. The right to know how your Medicare health plan pays its doctors. If you request information on how a Medicare health plan pays its doctors, the plan must give it to you in writing. You also have the right to know whether your doctor has a financial interest in a health care facility, such as a laboratory, since it could affect the medical advice he or she gives you.

7. The right to choose a women's health specialist.

8. The right, if you have a complex or serious medical condition, to receive a treatment plan that includes direct access to a specialist.

If you believe that any of your rights have been violated, please call the State Health Insurance Assistance Program in your State.*

* Source: Social Security Administration.

APPENDIX 21: INFORMED CONSENT TO PERFORM AN HIV TEST

DOH

Informed Consent to Perform an HIV Test

New York State Department of Health
AIDS Institute

The decision to have an HIV test is voluntary. In order to have an HIV test in New York State, you must give your consent in writing on the bottom of this form.

Testing for HIV Infection

Testing Methods:

There are a number of tests that can be done to show if you are infected with HIV, the virus that causes AIDS. Your provider or counselor can provide specific information on these tests. These tests involve collecting and testing blood, urine or oral fluid. The most common test for HIV is the HIV antibody test.

Meaning of HIV Test Results:

- A negative result on the HIV antibody test most likely means that you are not infected with HIV, but it may not show recent infection. If you think you have been exposed to HIV, you should take the test again three months after the last possible exposure.
- A positive result on the test means that you are infected with HIV and can infect others.
- Sometimes the HIV antibody test result is not clearly positive or negative, or may be a preliminary result. Your provider or counselor will explain this result, and may ask that you give your consent for further testing.

Confidential or Anonymous HIV Testing:

When you decide to have an HIV antibody test, you may choose either a confidential or an anonymous test.

- If you want your test result to become part of your medical record so it can be used for your medical care, you can have a confidential test done. A confidential test requires that you provide your name.
- If you do not want anyone to know your test results or that you were tested, you can have an anonymous test at an anonymous test site. You will not be asked your name, address or any other identifying information.
- If you receive an HIV positive test result at an anonymous test site approved by the NYS Department of Health, you will have the option of changing your test result to confidential by attaching your name to the test result. This will allow your test result to become part of your medical record.

Benefits to Testing:

There are many benefits to having an HIV test and knowing if you are infected.

If you receive an HIV negative test result:

- Your provider or counselor will tell you how to protect yourself from getting infected with HIV in the future.

If you receive an HIV positive test result:

- Your provider can give you medical care and treatment that can help you stay healthy and can manage your HIV illness.
- Your provider or counselor can tell you how to prevent passing the virus to your sexual or needle sharing partners.
- You can increase your chances of staying healthy by eating a well-balanced, nutritious diet, getting enough sleep, exercising, avoiding alcohol, tobacco, and recreational drugs, reducing stress and having regular check-ups.

If you are a woman who receives an HIV positive test result:

- If you are thinking about having a child, your provider will give you information to help you make informed choices about your health care and pregnancy.
- If you are pregnant, your doctor can provide the care you need and information about services and options available to you. Your provider can tell you about the risks of passing HIV infection to your baby, about medications given during pregnancy that can significantly reduce the risk of passing HIV to your baby, and the medical care available for babies who may be infected with HIV.
- If you have given birth to or breast fed a child since you were infected, your child will need to be tested for HIV and, if infected, may need additional care and treatment. Your provider can give you information about medical care available for children who may be infected with HIV.

DOH-2556 (p. 1 of 2) Informed Consent to Perform an HIV Test (English) **(Rev. 6/00)**

Confidentiality of HIV Information:

If you take the HIV antibody test, your test results are confidential. Under New York State law, confidential HIV information can only be given to people you allow to have it by giving your written approval, or to people who need to know your HIV status in order to provide medical care and services, including: medical care providers; persons involved with foster care or adoption; parents and guardians who consent to care of minors; jail, prison, probation and parole employees; emergency response workers and other workers in hospitals, other regulated settings or medical offices, who are exposed to blood/body fluids in the course of their employment; and organizations that review the services you receive. The law also allows your HIV information to be released under limited circumstances: by special court order; to public health officials as required by law; and to insurers as necessary to pay for care and treatment.

Reporting Requirements:

Your name will be reported to the health department if you have a confirmed positive HIV antibody test result received through a confidential test, other HIV-related test results, a diagnosis of AIDS, or if you have chosen to attach your name to a positive test result at an anonymous site. The health department will use this information to track the epidemic and to better plan prevention, health care and other services.

Notifying Partners:

If you test HIV positive, your provider will talk with you about the importance and benefits of notifying your partners of their possible exposure to HIV. It is important that your partners know they may have been exposed to HIV so they can find out whether they are infected and benefit from early diagnosis and treatment. Your provider may ask you to provide the names of your partners, and whether it is safe for you if they are notified. If you have been in an abusive relationship with one of these partners, it is important to share information with your provider. For information regarding services related to domestic violence, call 1-800-942-6906.

- Under state law, your provider is required to report to the health department the names of any of your partners (present and past sexual partners, including spouses, and needle sharing partners) whom they know.
- If you have additional partners whom your provider does not know, you may give their names to your provider so they can be notified.
- Several options are available to assist you and your provider in notifying partners. If you or your provider do not have a plan to notify your partners, the Health Department may notify them without revealing your identity. If this notification presents a risk of harm to you, the Health Department may defer the notification for a period of time sufficient to allow you to access domestic violence prevention services.
- If you do not name any partners to your provider or if a need exists to confirm information about your partners, the health department may contact you to request your cooperation in this process.

Confidentiality of HIV Test Results and Related Information:

If you feel your confidentiality has been broken, or for more information about HIV confidentiality, call the New York State Department of Health HIV Confidentiality Hotline at 1-800-962-5065. Any health or social service provider who illegally tells anyone about your HIV information may be punished by a fine of up to $5,000 and a jail term of up to one year. The law also protects you from HIV-related discrimination in housing, employment, health care or other services. For more information, call the New York State Division of Human Rights at 1-800-523-2437.

My questions about the HIV antibody test were answered. I agree to be tested for HIV.

Signature: ______________________________

Date: ______________________________

I provided pre-test counseling in accordance with Article 27-F of the New York State Public Health Law. I answered the above individual's questions about the test and offered him/her an unsigned copy of this form.

Signature:______________________________Title:______________________________

Facility/Provider Name:______________________________

DOH-2556 (p. 2 of 2) Informed Consent to Perform an HIV Test (English) **(Rev. 6/00)**

APPENDIX 22: TABLE OF STATE LAWS CONCERNING ISSUES RELATED TO HIV TESTING

STATE	STATUTE	PROVISIONS
Alabama	N/A	no statutory provisions
Alaska	N/A	no statutory provisions,
Arizona	Arizona Revised Statutes Annotated, §36-663	prior written informed consent
Arkansas	Arkansas Statutes Annotated, §20-15-901	testing is confidential
California	California Health and Safety Code, §199.22(a)	prior written informed consent
Colorado	N/A	no statutory provisions
Connecticut	Connecticut General Statutes Annotated, §19a-582	prior informed consent
Delaware	Delaware Code Annotated, Title 16, §1203	prior written informed consent except following health care worker exposure or to control sexually transmitted disease
District of Columbia	N/A	no statutory provisions
Florida	Florida Statutes Annotated, §381.609(2)(e)	prior written informed consent
Georgia	Code of Georgia, §31-17A-2; 15-11-35.1; 42-5-52.1; 31-22-9.2; 31-17A-3	see statutes for conditions which vary according to applicable statutes governing, e.g. minors, prison inmates, etc.

STATE	STATUTE	PROVISIONS
Hawaii	Hawaii Revised Statutes, §325-16	Prior written informed consent
Idaho	N/A	no statutory provisions
Illinois	Illinois Revised Statutes, Chapter 111-1/2, Para 7305	prior written informed consent
Indiana	Indiana Code Annotated, §16-1-9.5-2.5	prior informed consent
Iowa	Code of Iowa, §141.22	prior notice that testing is voluntary
Kansas	N/A	no statutory provisions
Kentucky	Kentucky Revised Statutes, §311.281	prior informed written consent of prospective tissue donors
Louisiana	Louisiana Revised Statutes,§40.1229.40(D)	testing without consent if hospital employees exposed to patient's blood or bodily fluids
Maine	Maine Revised Statutes Annotated, Title 5, §19203-A	prior written informed consent
Maryland	Maryland Health General Code Annotated, §18-213	emergency rescue personnel entitled to notification when rescued person subsequently diagnosed as having a contagious disease
Massachusetts	Massachusetts Annotated Laws Chapter 11, §70F	prior written informed consent
Michigan	N/A	no statutory provisions
Minnesota	Minnesota Statutes Annotated, §144.762	counseling prior to testing
Mississippi	N/A	no statutory provisions
Missouri	Annotated Missouri Statutes, §191.653	consultation required prior to testing and upon receipt of results
Montana	Revised Montana Code Annotated, §15-16-1007	prior written informed consent

STATE	STATUTE	PROVISIONS
Nebraska	N/A	no statutory provisions
Nevada	Nevada Revised Statutes, §441A.320	required on perpetrator of crime involving sexual penetration
New Hampshire	New Hampshire Revised Statutes Annotated, §141-F:5	prior informed consent
New Jersey	New Jersey Revised Statutes Annotated, §26:5C-6; 26:5C-8	anonymous and confidential
New Mexico	New Mexico Statutes Annotated, §24-2B-2; 24-2B-3	prior informed consent and counseling for recipients of positive test results
New York	N/A	informed consent
North Carolina	N/A	no statutory provisions
North Dakota	N/A	no statutory provisions
Ohio	N/A	no statutory provisions
Oklahoma	N/A	no statutory provisions
Oregon	Oregon Revised Statutes, §433.045	prior consent unless approval by Commissioner of Health for research with confidentiality provision
Pennsylvania	N/A	no statutory provisions,
Rhode Island	Rhode Island General Laws, §23-6-12	prior written informed consent
South Carolina	N/A	no statutory provisions,
South Dakota	N/A	no statutory provisions
Tennessee	N/A	no statutory provisions
Texas	Texas Civil Practice Code Annotated, §902(a)	counseling for recipients of positive test results
Utah	N/A	no statutory provisions
Vermont	N/A	no statutory provisions
Virginia	Code of Virginia Annotated, §32.1-37.2	prior informed consent

STATE	STATUTE	PROVISIONS
Washington	Washington Revised Code, §70.24.701	consent required unless subject convicted of sexual offense, prostitution or related offenses, or IV drug-related offenses, or at request of emergency medical technicians or others substantially exposed to blood or fluids of emergency victim
West Virginia	West Virginia Code, §16-3C-2	prior consent
Wisconsin	Wisconsin Statutes Annotated, §146.025	prior written informed consent, counseling for recipient of positive test results, disclosure of results permitted to health care provider caring for subject, funeral director or persons who autopsy subject; emergency caregivers significantly exposed to subject; and coroners or medical examiners if information relevant to determine cause of death or if significantly exposed to subject
Wyoming	N/A	no statutory provisions

APPENDIX 23: INFORMED CONSENT TO PERFORM AN EXPEDITED HIV TEST IN THE DELIVERY SETTING

New York State Department of Health

Informed Consent to Perform an Expedited HIV Test in the Delivery Setting

(Please note: Either this form or the standard HIV form can be used to consent to an expedited test.)

HIV testing is voluntary and requires your consent in writing. The purpose of expedited HIV testing is to show if you are infected with HIV, the virus that causes AIDS. **If you are HIV-infected, expedited HIV testing will allow you to receive immediate medication during labor and delivery to reduce the risk of transmitting HIV to your newborn, and will allow your baby to receive the same medication immediately after birth.**

Before you consent to be tested for HIV, speak to your health care provider about:
How HIV can be passed from person to person and mother to baby;
The medication that has been shown in many cases to prevent the transmission of HIV from mother to baby;
The New York State law that requires all newborns to be tested for HIV after birth (without the parents' consent); and,
The meaning of preliminary HIV test results and how a positive HIV test will be confirmed.

If you agree with the following statements and want to consent to expedited HIV testing, please sign on the other side of this form.

I have been counseled about the benefits of having an expedited HIV test and I understand that HIV infection can be passed from mother to baby.

I understand that:

- The human immunodeficiency virus (HIV) is the virus that causes AIDS.
- One of the ways that HIV is spread is by sexual intercourse, so all pregnant women are potentially at risk for HIV infection.
- HIV can be passed from a mother to her baby during pregnancy, at delivery, and through breastfeeding.
- If I have HIV, it is a serious illness that can affect my health and the health of my baby.
- HIV antibody test results are confidential and the law protects me from discrimination related to HIV.

If I am found to be HIV-infected, treatment is available to reduce the risk that my baby will be infected:

- If I have not yet delivered my baby, I may receive medication as soon as possible which may greatly reduce the chance of my passing the virus to my baby.
- My baby may receive medication which reduces the risk of his/her becoming HIV-infected.
- If medication to reduce the risk of transmission of HIV is given to me during labor and delivery, or to my newborn immediately after birth, the chance that my baby will be HIV-infected is about 1 in 12. Without treatment, the chance that my baby will be infected is about 1 in 4.
- If treatment is started, my health care provider will discuss any consequences of taking the medication with me.

New York State has a Newborn Screening Program:

- If I do not consent to expedited testing now, my baby will be tested for HIV without consent immediately after birth.
- All babies born in New York State are also routinely tested for HIV as a part of the Newborn Screening Program; the test results are reported to their mothers.

The test I am consenting to take will provide me and my health care provider with results within 48 hours:

- If I have the expedited HIV test, I will be given the results no later than 48 hours after my blood is drawn.
- If the expedited HIV test result is negative, no further testing will be done at this time.
- If my expedited HIV test result is negative, it most likely means that I am not infected with HIV, but it may not show recent infection.
- A positive preliminary HIV test result means that there is a possibility that I am HIV-infected and that my baby may have been exposed to HIV. A second test, to confirm a preliminary positive HIV test result, will be done.
- I understand that if my preliminary test result is positive, I still may not have HIV infection (false positive tests can occur) but that it may be best to start treatment to help prevent the transmission of infection to my baby while I wait for the confirmatory test result.
- If my preliminary HIV test result is positive, my health care provider will advise me not to begin breastfeeding until the confirmatory test is done.

All preliminary positive test results will be confirmed:

- If the confirmatory HIV test result is negative, both my baby and I will immediately be taken off medication if it was started to help prevent transmission of HIV from me to my baby.
- If the confirmatory test is positive, any medication that was begun to help prevent transmission of HIV from me to my baby will be continued.
- If my confirmatory test is positive, further testing will be needed to determine whether or not my baby has HIV infection.
- If the confirmatory test is positive, I will be referred to a physician for my own ongoing medical care and I will be referred to a health care provider who will take care of my baby's medical needs.

DOH-4158 (Rev. 6/00) P. 1 of 2

Confidentiality of HIV Information:

If you take the HIV antibody test, your test results are confidential. Under New York State law, confidential HIV information can only be given to people you allow to have it by giving your written approval, or to people who need to know your HIV status in order to provide medical care and services, including: medical care providers; persons involved with foster care or adoption; parents and guardians who consent to care of minors; jail, prison, probation and parole employees; emergency response workers and other workers in hospitals, other regulated settings or medical offices, who are exposed to blood/body fluids in the course of their employment; and organizations that review the services you receive. The law also allows your HIV information to be released under certain limited circumstances: by special court order; to public health officials as required by law; and to insurers as necessary to pay for care and treatment.

Reporting Requirements:

Your name will be reported to the Health Department if you have a confirmed positive HIV antibody test result received through a confidential test, other HIV-related test results, a diagnosis of AIDS, or if you have chosen to attach your name to a positive test result at an anonymous site. The Health Department will use this information to track the epidemic and to better plan prevention, health care and other services.

Notifying Partners:

If you test HIV positive, your provider will talk with you about the importance and benefits of notifying your partners of their possible exposure to HIV. It is important that your partners know they may have been exposed to HIV so they can find out whether they are infected and benefit from early diagnosis and treatment. Your provider may ask you to provide the names of your partners, and whether it is safe for you if they are notified. If you have been in an abusive relationship with one of these partners, it is important to share information with your provider. For information regarding services related to domestic violence, call 1-800-942-6906.

- Under state law, your provider is required to report to the Health Department the names of any of your partners (present and past sexual partners, including spouses, and needle sharing partners) whom they know.
- If you have additional partners whom your provider does not know, you may give their names to your provider so they can be notified.
- Several options are available to assist you and your provider in notifying partners. If you or your provider do not have a plan to notify your partners, the Health Department may notify them without revealing your identity. If this notification presents a risk to you, the Health Department may defer the notification for a period of time sufficient to allow you to access domestic violence prevention services.
- If you do not name any partners to your provider or if a need exists to confirm information about your partners, the Health Department may contact you to request your cooperation in this process.

Confidentiality of HIV Test Results and Related Information:

If you feel your confidentiality has been broken, or for more information about HIV confidentiality, call the New York State Department of Health HIV Confidentiality Hotline at 1-800-962-5065. Any health or social service provider who illegally tells anyone about your HIV information may be punished by a fine of up to $5,000 and a jail term of up to one year. The law also protects you from HIV-related discrimination in housing, employment, health care or other services. For more information, call the New York State Division of Human Rights at 1-800-523-2437.

My questions about the HIV antibody test were answered. I agree to be tested for HIV.

Signature:______________________________

Date:_________________________________

I provided pre-test counseling in accordance with Article 27-F of the New York State Public Health Law. I answered the above individual's questions about the test and offered her an unsigned copy of this form.

Signature: ______________________________
Title:_________________________________
Facility/Provider
Name:____

DOH-4158 (Rev. 6/00) P.2 of 2 Informed Consent to Perform an Expedited HIV Test in the Delivery Setting

APPENDIX 24: TABLE OF STATE STATUTES CONCERNING HIV PARTNER NOTIFICATION

STATE, STATUTE	SUMMARY
Alabama Code §22-11A-38(d)	physicians or the state health official may notify a third party where there is a "foreseeable, real or probable risk of transmission of the disease."
Alabama Code §22-11A-38(f)	extends immunity from liability to physicians, health department employees, and hospitals and other health care facilities, for notifying or failing to notify partners exposed to infected person.
Alabama Code §22-11A-53	notification of positive HIV test result shall include an explanation of the benefits of locating, testing and counseling partners and a full description of the public health services for locating and counseling partners.
Arizona Revised Statutes §32-1457(A)/§32-1860(A)	a physician may report the name of the spouse or sex/needlesharing partner of a patient that has tested positive for HIV to the department of health services if: the physician knows that the patient has not or will not notify these people; and the physician has asked the patient to release this information voluntarily.
Arizona Revised Statutes §32-1457(C)/§32-1860(C)	extends immunity from liability to physicians for notifying or failing to notify partners exposed to infected person.

STATE, STATUTE	SUMMARY
Arizona Revised Statutes §36-664(K)	any person who knows that an individual is HIV positive, and who reasonably believes that an identifiable third party is at risk of HIV infection from that individual, may report that risk to the Health Department. Upon receipt of such report the department shall notify the person at risk.
Arizona Revised Statutes §36-665	an order for disclosure of or a search warrant for confidential communicable disease-related information may be issued on a showing of a clear and imminent danger to a person whose life or health may unknowingly be at significant risk as a result of contact with the person to whom the information pertains.
Arizona Revised Statutes §36-666(C)	extends immunity from civil or criminal liability to a health care facility or health care provider for failing to notify the contact of a person with a communicable disease.
California Health & Safety Code §121015	a physician may notify a person reasonably believed to be the spouse or sex/needle-sharing partner of a patient testing positive for HIV of their exposure to HIV if the physician has: discussed the test results with the patient and offered appropriate educational and psychological counseling; and notified the patient of the intent to notify patient's partners prior to notification. A physician has no duty to notify and may not be held criminally or civilly liable for notifying partners. A physician may also report risk of exposure to third parties to the health department, which may then alert those persons to their risk.
Colorado Revised Statutes §25-4-1405.5(2)(a)(II)	the state board of health shall adopt rules specifying the performance standards for anonymous and confidential counseling and testing, including standards for partner notification.

STATE, STATUTE	SUMMARY
Colorado Revised Statutes §25-4-1406	as a last resort, the executive director of the state department of public health, or the director of the local department of health may issue an order to direct a person with HIV infection to cease and desist from specified conduct which endangers the health of others.
Colorado Revised Statutes §25-4-1407	if the procedures of the previous section fail, the state executive director or local director may bring an action in district court to enjoin a person from engaging in specific conduct which endangers the public health. The district court may issue an order to take the person into custody for a period not to exceed seventy-two hours.
General Statutes of Connecticut §19a-584(a)	a public health officer may notify the partner of a person infected with HIV if: 1) she reasonably believes a significant risk of transmission exists, 2) she reasonably believes that the index patient will not himself warn the contact, and 3) she has informed the patient of her intent to warn the third party. The physician or public health officer has no obligation to warn, inform, identify or locate any partner.
General Statutes of Connecticut §19a-584(b)	a physician may notify a known partner of a patient who tests positive for HIV, if that partner is also a patient of the physician. A physician must follow the same procedures as public health officers before notifying a partner.
§19a-582(b)	anyone taking a test for HIV must be told before the test that if they test positive, public health counselors or a physician may notify their known partners of a risk of infection whether or not they have consent to do so.
Delaware Code §16-1203(a)(10)	allowing disclosure of HIV test results to a third party on court order based on "compelling need."

STATE, STATUTE	SUMMARY
Delaware Code §16-1205(c)	extends immunity from civil or criminal liability for disclosure of an HIV test result under §1203.
District of Columbia Code §6-117	a court may order disclosure of HIV status to a third person if it finds, upon clear and convincing evidence, that it is essential to safeguard the physical health of others. The person whose status is to be disclosed shall have an opportunity to contest the disclosure.
Florida Statutes §381.004(3)(e)	no HIV test result shall be revealed to the test subject without telling the subject the benefits of locating and counseling any individual that may have been exposed to HIV by the subject and of the availability of public health services to help locate and counsel partners.
Florida Statutes §381.004(3)(f)(9)	a court may order HIV test results disclosed to a third party on a showing of compelling need, and after weighing the privacy interest of the test subject and the public interest which may be disserved by disclosure which deters HIV testing or which may lead to discrimination.
Florida Statutes §381.004(4)(c)	each county health department shall provide counseling and testing on an anonymous basis, including informing clients of the availability of partner notification services and the benefits of such services.
Florida Statutes §384.26	permitting the health department to interview all HIV positive individuals for information regarding the identification and notification of partners.
Florida Statutes §455.674	a health practitioner shall not be civilly or criminally liable for disclosing confidential HIV information to a sex or needle-sharing partner of a patient testing positive for HIV if the practitioner first recommends that the patient notify the partner or refrain from risk activities, and the practitioner has told the patient of her intent to inform the partner. A practitioner is not liable for failing to disclose such information.

STATE, STATUTE	SUMMARY
Official Code of Georgia §24-9-47(g)	a physician may notify a spouse, sexual partner or child of a patient infected with HIV that the physician reasonably believes to be at risk of exposure. The physician must attempt to notify the patient that disclosure will be made.
Official Code of Georgia §24-9-47(h)(3)(B)	the Department of Human Resources may contact any person reasonably believed to be at risk of being infected with HIV to disclose their possible exposure to HIV.
Official Code of Georgia §24-9-47(h)(3)(C)	the Department of Human Resources must contact and inform the spouse of an HIV infected person of their exposure if they are reasonably likely to have engaged in risk activities with the infected person.
Official Code of Georgia §24-9-47(j)	extends immunity from civil or criminal liability for authorized disclosure to third parties. Releases persons authorized to make disclosures from duty to disclose or liability for failing to disclose exposure to HIV to third parties.
Hawaii Code §325-101(a)(4)	physicians and public health officers may notify sex or needle-sharing partners of an HIV positive patient where: 1) there is reason to believe that the contact is at risk of HIV transmission; and 2) the patient has been counseled and is unwilling to inform the contact directly or consent to disclosure by a third person. Physicians and public health officers have no obligation to identify or locate any contact and are immune from civil or criminal liability.
Idaho Code §39-610(2)	state or local health authorities may contact and advise people who authorities believe to have been exposed to HIV.
Idaho Code §39-610(5)	extends immunity for civil or criminal liability for authorized disclosure or for nondisclosure.

STATE, STATUTE	SUMMARY
Illinois Compiled Statutes §410-305-9	a physician may notify the spouse of a patient who tests positive for HIV if the physician has tried to persuade the patient to notify the spouse or if, after a patient has agreed to make the notification the physician has reason to believe that the patient has not provided the notification. This section does not create a duty or obligation for a physician to notify the spouse, and no civil or criminal liability may be imposed on the physician for disclosing or failing to disclose HIV test results to a spouse.
Illinois Compiled Statutes §410-325-5.5	when the department of public health determines that a person infected with HIV may be exposing others to HIV, the department shall investigate the person with HIV and her contacts and notify the contacts if it appears that the person with HIV will not carry out notification.
Indiana Statutes §16-41-7-1	a person who is infected with HIV has a duty to warn or cause to be warned by a third party people with whom they are engaged in activities that carry a high risk of transmission of HIV.
Indiana Statutes §16-41-7-3(a)	a physician must inform patients with HIV of their duty to notify partners.
Indiana Statutes §16-41-7-3(b)(1)	a physician may notify a health officer of patients with HIV that pose a serious and present danger to the health of others, patients suspected of being at risk, or any other person reasonably believed to be at risk of contracting HIV.
Indiana Statutes §16-41-7-3(b)(2)	a physician may also notify persons at risk directly if she has reason to believe that they have been exposed to HIV, that they will not be informed by any other person, and she has made reasonable efforts to inform the patient of her intent to notify the person at risk.
Indiana Statutes §16-41-7-3(d)	a physician who provides notification in good faith is immune from civil or criminal liability.

STATE, STATUTE	SUMMARY
Indiana Statutes §16-41-7-4	a health officer or the state department shall notify persons reported to be at risk unless they determine that intervention is not necessary.
Code of Iowa §141.6(3)(a)	department of public health shall provide for a person who tests positive for HIV to receive counseling and be encouraged to refer partners for notification.
Code of Iowa §141.6(3)(d)(2)	when a physician believes that a patient infected with HIV will not warn a third party at risk, and will not participate in the voluntary partner notification program, she may reveal the identity of the patient to the extent necessary to protect the party at risk. The physician shall attempt to notify the infected patient of her intent to notify, the person to be notified, and the anticipated date of disclosure.
Kansas Statutes §65-6004	a physician who has reason to believe that the spouse or partner of a person who has tested positive for HIV has been exposed to HIV and is unaware of their exposure, may inform them of their risk of exposure. Such disclosure is immune from civil or criminal liability, and no duty to warn is created.
Louisiana Statutes §1300.14(E)	a physician may notify contacts of a patient infected with HIV if: she reasonably believes there is a significant risk of transmission to the contact; if the patient has been counseled and the physician reasonably believes that the patient will not inform the contact; and the physician has informed the patient of her intent to notify the contact. The physician has no obligation to identify or locate any contact.

STATE, STATUTE	SUMMARY
Louisiana Statutes §1300.15	a court may grant an order for disclosure of HIV test results to a third person upon a showing of a "clear and imminent danger to an individual whose life or health may unknowingly be at significant risk" as a result of contact with an individual whose HIV status is sought. "The court shall weigh the need for disclosure against the privacy interest of the protected individual and against the public interest that may not be served by disclosure which deters future testing or treatment or which may lead to discrimination."
Maine Revised Statutes §19203-D(A)	HIV infection status may be released only if the person to whom the information pertains has specifically authorized a separate release of that information. A general release form is insufficient.
Maine Revised Statutes §801	a person who fails or refuses to cooperate with a health department contact notification program, or who engages in behavior that creates a significant risk of transmission of a communicable disease is considered a "public health threat."
Maine Revised Statutes §808	a public health department investigative team shall have access to medical and laboratory records relevant to the investigation of a public health threat
Maine Revised Statutes §810	upon a showing of clear and convincing evidence that a person requires immediate custody in order to avoid a clear and immediate public health threat, a judge of the district court may grant temporary custody of the person and may order specific emergency care, treatment or evaluation.
Maryland Health-General Code §18-336(b)(2)	counseling before HIV testing must include informing the test subject of the physician's duty to warn third parties who may be at risk of contracting HIV from the subject.

STATE, STATUTE	SUMMARY
Maryland Health-General Code §18-337(b)	if an individual tests positive for HIV and refuses to notify her sex/needlesharing partners, the individual's physician may inform the local health officer and/or the individual's partners directly, of the identity of the HIV-positive patient and the circumstances giving rise to the notification. A physician may not be held liable for disclosure or nondisclosure if acting in good faith.
Michigan Statutes Annotated §14.15(5131)(5)(b)	creates an affirmative duty for a physician or local health officer to notify known partners of individuals infected with HIV or diagnosed as having AIDS, if the physical or health officer determines that notification is necessary to prevent a reasonably foreseeable risk of transmission of HIV.
Michigan Statutes Annotated §14.15(5131)(6)	a person who releases information in the course of partner notification is immune from civil or criminal liability.
Michigan Statutes Annotated §14.15(5131)(7)	a person who notifies a partner of an HIV infected individual shall not include information that identifies the infected individual unless the identifying information is determined by the person making the disclosure to be reasonably necessary to prevent a foreseeable risk of transmission of HIV.
Michigan Statutes Annotated §14.15(5114a)(1)	a person or government entity that administers a test for HIV shall refer individuals testing positive for assistance with partner notification if they determine that the individual needs assistance with partner notification
Michigan Statutes Annotated §14.15(5114a)(3)	a local health department that assists individuals with partner notification must inform the individual that he has a legal obligation to inform each of his sexual partners of his infection before engaging in sexual relations with that partner, and that he may be subject to criminal sanctions for failure to so inform his partners.

STATE, STATUTE	SUMMARY
Michigan Statutes Annotated §14.15(5114a)(5)	if a local health department receives a report that indicates that a resident of the state is HIV infected, the health department shall make it a priority to attempt to interview the individual and offer to contact the individual's sex/needle-sharing partners, and within 35 days of interview to contact each individual identified as a partner.
Revised Statutes of Missouri §191.656(2)(1)(d)	unless a person acts in bad faith or with conscious disregard, no person will be liable for violating any duty or right of confidentiality for disclosing the results of an individual's HIV testing to the spouse of the subject of the test.
Revised Statutes of Missouri §191.656(2)(2)	paragraph (d) does not impose any duty to disclose HIV testing results.
Revised Statutes of Missouri §191.656(6)	a person who negligently violates this section is liable for actual damages, injunctive relief, court costs and reasonable attorney's fees, and a person who willfully or intentionally or recklessly violates this section is liable for the same damages and for exemplary damages.
Revised Statutes of Missouri §191.686(4)	all anonymous test sites are required to initiate partner notification when submitting test results to individuals who test positive for HIV.
Montana Code Annotated §50-16-1009(3)	a health care provider shall encourage a subject testing positive for HIV to notify potential contacts. If the subject is unable or unwilling to notify contacts, the health care provider may ask the subject to disclose voluntarily the identities of the contacts and to authorize notification of the contacts by a health care provider.
Montana Code Annotated §50-16-529(9)	a health care provider may disclose health care information about a patient, without the patient's authorization, to any contact if the health care provider reasonably believes that disclosure will avoid or minimize an imminent danger to the health or safety of the contact or any other individual.

STATE, STATUTE	SUMMARY
Montana Code Annotated §50-16-1004	expressing the intent of the legislature to treat AIDS and HIV infection in the same manner as other communicable diseases, including sexually transmitted diseases, by adopting the most currently accepted public health practices with regard to, among other things, partner notification.
Montana Code Annotated §50-18-106	if a physician or other person knows or has reason to suspect that a person who has a sexually transmitted disease is conducting himself in a way which might expose another to infection, he shall immediately notify the local health officer of the name and address of the diseased person and the essential facts in the case.
Revised Statutes of Nebraska §71-501.02(6)	to the extent funds are available, the Department of Health and Human Services may offer partner notification services that are culturally and language specific upon request to persons testing positive for HIV.
Nevada Revised Statutes Annotated §441A.220(5)	confidential information about a communicable disease may be disclosed to any person who has a medical need to know the information for his own protection or for the well-being of a patient or dependent person.
New Jersey Statutes §26:5C-9(a)	the record of a person who has or is suspected of having AIDS or HIV infection may be disclosed by an order of a court upon a showing of good cause. At a good cause hearing the court shall weigh the public interest and need for disclosure against injury to the person who is the subject of the record, to the physician-patient relationship, and to the services offered by the program.
New Mexico Statutes Annotated §24-1-8	if a physician knows or has good reason to suspect that a person with an STD may conduct himself so as to expose other persons to infection, he shall notify the district health officer of the name and address of the diseased person and the facts of the case.

STATE, STATUTE	SUMMARY
New Mexico Statutes Annotated §24-2B-4	a person who tests positive for HIV must be informed of the benefits of locating and counseling any partners that may have been exposed to HIV.
New York Consolidated Law Services—Public Health Law §2782(4)(a)	a physician may disclose confidential HIV-related information to a contact or to a public health officer for disclosure to a contact if: the physician reasonably believes there is a significant risk of infection to the contact; the physician has counseled the patient infected with HIV of the need to notify the contact; the physician reasonably believes the patient will not inform the contact; and the physician has informed the patient of her intent to notify the contact.
New York Consolidated Law Services—Public Health Law §2782(4)(c)	a physician or public health officer has no obligation to identify or locate any contact.
New York Consolidated Law Services - Public Health Law §2785(2)(b)	a court may grant an order for disclosure of confidential HIV-related information upon a showing of clear and imminent danger to an individual whose life or health may unknowingly be at significant risk as a result of contact with the individual to whom the information pertains.
New York Consolidated Law Services—Public Health Law §2785(5)	in assessing compelling need and clear and imminent danger, the court shall weigh the need for disclosure against the privacy interest of the protected individual and the public interest which may be disserved by disclosure which deters future testing or treatment or which may lead to discrimination.
General Statutes of North Carolina §130A-143(4)	information relating to the HIV status of an individual may be released if necessary to protect the public health and is made as provided by the Commission in its rules regarding control measures for communicable diseases.

STATE, STATUTE	SUMMARY
North Dakota Century Code §23-07.4-01(2)(c)	when a state health officer knows, or has reason to believe that a person has HIV and is a danger to the public health, and the infected person has been ordered to report for counseling and information on how to avoid infecting others, that official may issue an order to direct that person to cease and desist from specified conduct that endangers the health of others.
North Dakota Century Code §23-07.4-01(4)	If a court affirms the order, and the person subject to the order is infected with HIV, the court shall require the person to disclose the names and addresses of sex/needle-sharing partners. Failure to comply with court-ordered disclosure constitutes contempt of court.
North Dakota Century Code §23-07.4-02	if the procedures of the previous section have been exhausted, and a person believed to be infected with HIV continues to engage in behavior that presents an imminent danger to the public health, a court may issue other orders, including an order to take the person into custody, for a period not to exceed 90 days and place the person in a facility designated or approved by the state health officer.
Ohio Revised Code Annotated §3701.241(A)	the director of public health shall develop and administer both confidential and anonymous tests for HIV and a confidential partner notification system.
Ohio Revised Code Annotated §3701-241(B)	the director shall prepare a list of sites where an individual may obtain an anonymous HIV test, and make available a copy of the list to anyone who requests it.

STATE, STATUTE	SUMMARY
Ohio Revised Code Annotated §3701.243(C)(1)(b)	a court may issue an order granting access to or authority to disclose HIV test results only if the court finds by clear and convincing evidence that there is a compelling need for disclosure. The court shall weigh the need for disclosure against the privacy right of the individual tested and against any disservice to the public interest that might result from the disclosure, such as discrimination against the individual or the deterrence of others from being tested.
Ohio Revised Code Annotated §3701.243(F)	an individual who knows that he is HIV positive shall disclose this information to any other person with whom he intends to have sex or share a hypodermic needle.
Oklahoma Statutes §1-502.2	confidential information about a person with a communicable disease may be released if necessary to protect the health and well-being of the general public.
Oregon Revised Statutes §433.008	if the local public health administrator determines that a person with a contagious disease is violating the rules of the division pertaining to control of that disease, it may disclose that person's name and address to a third person if clear and convincing evidence requires disclosure to avoid a clear and immediate danger to other individuals or to the public generally. A decision not to disclose information, if made in good faith, shall not subject the person withholding the information to liability.
Pennsylvania Statutes §7609(A)	a physician may disclose confidential HIV-related information to a known contact of a patient infected with HIV if: the physician reasonably believes disclosure is medically appropriate and there is a significant risk of future infection to the contact; the physician has counseled the patient about the need to notify the contact and the physician reasonably believes the patient will not inform the contact or abstain from activities which pose a significant risk of infection to the contact.

STATE, STATUTE	SUMMARY
Pennsylvania Statutes §7609(B)	a physician shall have no duty to identify, locate or notify any contact and no cause of action shall arise for nondisclosure or for disclosure.
Pennsylvania Statutes §7608	a court may issue an order to allow access to confidential HIV related information upon a showing of compelling need.
General Laws of Rhode Island §23-6-17(2)(v)	a physician may disclose the HIV-positive status of a patient to a third party who has contact with that patient if there is a clear and present danger of HIV transmission to the third party, and if, despite the physician's strong encouragement, the patient has not and will not warn the third party.
South Carolina Annotated §44-29-146	a physician or state agency identifying and notifying a spouse or known contact of a person having HIV is not liable for damages resulting from the disclosure.
South Carolina Annotated §44-29-90	the Department of Health and Environmental Control must, to the extent resources are available, notify known sex/needle-sharing contacts of a person who has HIV.
South Dakota Codified Laws §34-22-9(3)	the department of health shall establish procedures for communicable disease contact notification, referral and management.
South Dakota Codified Laws §34-22-12.1	confidential information about a communicable disease may be disclosed to the extent necessary to protect the health or life of a named person.
Tennessee Code Annotated §68-5-101	whenever any case of communicable disease exists or is suspected to exist in any household, it is the duty of the head of the household, or any other person in the household possessing knowledge of the facts, to notify the municipal or county health authorities.

STATE, STATUTE	SUMMARY
Tennessee Code Annotated §68-10-115	a person who has a reasonable belief that a person has knowingly exposed another to HIV may inform the potential victim without incurring any liability.
Texas Health & Safety Code §81-051(g)(1)	a partner notification program shall notify the partner of a person with HIV infection with or without the consent of the person with HIV.
Texas Health & Safety Code §81-051(g)(2)	a health care professional shall notify the partner notification program when the health care professional knows the HIV status of a patient and has actual knowledge of possible transmission of HIV to a third party.
Texas Health & Safety Code §81-051-(h)	a health care professional who fails to make the notification required by section (g) is immune from civil or criminal liability.
Utah Code Annotated §26-63.5	the department of health shall utilize contact tracing and other methods for partner identification and notification.
Virginia Code Annotated §32.1-36.1	the results of a test for HIV may be released to the spouse of the person tested.
Virginia Code Annotated §32.1-37.2	every person who tests for HIV shall be informed of the need to notify any partners who may have been exposed to the virus.
Revised Code of Washington §70.24.105(f)	a court may order disclosure of an HIV test to a third party on a showing of good cause and weighing the public interest and the need for disclosure against the injury to the patient, to the physician patient relationship, and to the treatment services.
Revised Code of Washington §70.24.105(h)	if a health officer determines that a person has been placed at risk of contracting HIV, and that the exposed person is unaware of the risk, then the identity of the person with HIV that they are in contact with may be disclosed.

STATE, STATUTE	SUMMARY
West Virginia Code §16-3C-3(d)	sex or needle-sharing partners of a person with HIV may be notified of their exposure to HIV without revealing the identity of the person with HIV, and no cause of action may arise from such notification.
West Virginia Code §16-3C-3(e)	a physician or health care provider has no duty to notify the spouse or other sex or needle-sharing partner of a person infected with HIV, and no cause of action may arise from the failure to notify.
Wisconsin Statutes §252.12	the public health department shall contact individuals who test positive for HIV and encourage them to refer any sex or needle-sharing partners for counseling and testing.
Wyoming Statutes §35-4-133	a health officer shall make every reasonable effort to notify any sex or needlesharing partners of a person with a sexually transmitted disease (including HIV) of their possible exposure to infection. *

* Source: American Civil Liberties Union, 2000.

APPENDIX 25: SELECTED PROVISIONS OF THE MODEL STATE PUBLIC HEALTH PRIVACY ACT

PREFATORY NOTES

The purpose of the Model State Public Health Privacy Act project is to develop a model state law [hereinafter the "Act"] addressing privacy and security issues arising from the acquisition, use, disclosure, and storage of identifiable health information by public health agencies at the state and local levels. The Act regulates the acquisition, use, disclosure, and storage of identifiable, health-related information by public health agencies without significantly limiting the ability of agencies to use such information for legitimate public health purposes.

ARTICLE I: FINDINGS AND DEFINITIONS

Section 1-101. Legislative Findings

The [State Legislative Body] finds that:

(1) Public health agencies acquire, use, disclose, or store an increasing amount of health-related information about individuals, some of which is highly-sensitive, in paper-based and electronic forms for legitimate public health purposes;

(2) Uses of health-related information for legitimate public health purposes are critically important to preserving, monitoring, and improving population-based health as well as personal health of individuals;

(3) Individuals have significant privacy interests with respect to health-related information which can be identified to them;

(4) Individual privacy interests in health-related information justify duties and limitations concerning (a) the acquisition, use, disclosure, and storage of such information; (b) individual access to such

information in the possession of public health agencies; and (c) security protections for such information;

(5) Individual interests in the privacy of health-related information are significantly reduced when the information is acquired, used, disclosed, or stored in non-identifiable forms;

(6) Public health agencies have a significant interest in protecting the privacy of health-related information in their possession where protecting the privacy of such information encourages individuals to participate in public health programs and objectives; and

(7) While public health agencies generally have an excellent record of protecting the privacy interests of individuals in health-related information possessed by the agencies, additional statutory protections will further clarify and protect individual privacy interests while facilitating, without jeopardizing, legitimate public health purposes.

Section 1-102. Purposes

The [State Legislative Body] states that the purposes of this Act are to:

(1) Address privacy and security issues arising from the acquisition, use, disclosure, and storage of protected health information by public health agencies at the State and local levels;

(2) Protect health-related information in the possession of public health agencies against unauthorized disclosures without significantly limiting the ability of agencies to use such information for legitimate public health purposes;

(3) Encourage wide use and disclosure of non-identifiable health information because this information does not implicate privacy and security concerns at the individual level and may greatly facilitate the accomplishment of legitimate public health purposes;

(4) Require the acquisition and uses of protected health information to be consistent with legitimate public health purposes;

(5) Prohibit disclosures of protected health information without the informed consent of the individual who is the subject of the information, with specified, narrow exceptions;

(6) Impose the duty on public health agencies to hold and use protected health information securely;

(7) Impose a general duty on public health agencies to ensure the accuracy of protected health information;

(8) Allow individuals access to their protected health information in the possession of public health agencies through inspection and copying privileges;

(9) Provide individuals the opportunity to request the correction, amendment, or deletion of erroneous, incomplete, or false protected health information; and

(10) Prescribe various criminal penalties and civil enforcement mechanisms to protect individuals who are harmed by violations of the Act by public health agencies, public health officials, and other persons.

Section 1-103. Definitions [Omitted]

ARTICLE II: ACQUISITION OF PROTECTED HEALTH INFORMATION

Section 2-101. Acquisition of Protected Health Information

[a] In General. A public health agency shall only acquire protected health information where:

(1) the acquisition relates directly to a legitimate public health purpose;

(2) the acquisition is reasonably likely to achieve such purpose, taking into account the provisions of this Act and other governing laws, and the availability of resources or means to achieve such purpose; and

(3) the legitimate public health purpose cannot otherwise be achieved as well or better with non-identifiable information.

[b] Secret Acquisition. Protected health information shall not be secretly acquired by a public health agency.

[c] Public Notice Requirements. Prior to implementation of a public health agency determination to acquire or store protected health information, the agency shall announce, through public notice and comment, and through public written notice distributed and posted in a manner and to such extent as will reasonably inform members of the affected community, its intentions to acquire or store protected health information and the purposes for which the information will be used. Such notice shall not identify any individual who is or may be the subject of protected health information. Where State or local law requires counseling services regarding a reportable disease, such counseling services shall include information that such disease is reportable to the

public health agency and a description of the purposes for which the individual's protected health information will be used by such agency.

Section 2-102. Subsequent Acquisition of Protected Health Information

A public health agency shall not acquire protected health information from another local, State, or federal public health agency unless the acquisition is consistent with the requirements of Section 2-101.

ARTICLE III: USES OF PROTECTED HEALTH INFORMATION

Section 3-101. Uses Consistent With Original Legitimate Public Health Purposes

[a] In General. Protected health information shall be used by a public health agency solely for legitimate public health purposes that are directly related to the purpose for which the information was acquired. Providing access to protected health information to any person other than a public health agency or public health official is not a use.

[b] Subsequent Uses. A public health agency may use protected health information for legitimate public health purposes that are not directly related to the purpose for which the information was acquired provided that the agency meets the requirements of Section 2-101[a] and [c] before using such information.

[c] Research Use. A public health agency or official may use protected health information for public health, epidemiological, medical, or health services research provided that:

(1) it is not feasible to obtain the informed consent of the individual who is the subject of the information;

(2) identifiable information is necessary for the effectiveness of the research project;

(3) the minimum amount of information necessary to conduct the research is used;

(4) the research utilizing the protected health information will likely contribute to achieving a legitimate public health purpose;

(5) the information is made non-identifiable at the earliest opportunity consistent with the purposes of the research project and expunged after the conclusion of the project; and

(6) such uses are made pursuant to assurances of protections through the execution of a confidentiality agreement after review

and approval of an institutional review board. The agreement shall require any person receiving such information to adhere to protections for the privacy and security of the information equivalent to or greater than such protections provided in this Act.

Section 3-102. Scope of Uses

[a] In General. Non-identifiable health information shall be used by a public health agency whenever possible consistent with the accomplishment of legitimate public health purposes.

[b] Minimum Information. Any use of protected health information permitted by this Act shall be limited to the minimum amount of information which the public health official using the information reasonably believes is necessary to accomplish the legitimate public health purpose.

Section 3-103. Commercial Uses

Protected health information shall not be used by a public health agency or public health official for commercial purposes.

Section 3-104. De-identifying Protected Health Information

Protected health information whose use by a public health agency no longer furthers the legitimate public health purpose for which it was acquired shall be expunged in a confidential manner.

ARTICLE IV: DISCLOSURES OF PROTECTED HEALTH INFORMATION

Section 4-101. Non-Public Information

Protected health information is not public information, and may not be disclosed without the informed consent of the individual (or the individual's lawful representative) who is the subject of the information, except as provided in this Act.

Section 4-102. Informed Consent

[a] Generally. For the purposes of this Act, informed consent means a written authorization for the disclosure of protected health information on a form substantially similar to one promulgated by the [State public health agency] which is signed in writing or electronically by the individual who is the subject of the information. This authorization shall be dated and shall specify to whom the disclosure is authorized, the gen-

eral purpose for such disclosure, and the time period in which the authorization for the disclosure is effective.

[b] Revocation. An individual may revoke an authorization in writing at any time. The individual is responsible for informing the person who originally received the authorization that it has been revoked.

[c] Expiration. If the authorization does not contain an expiration date or has not previously been revoked, it automatically expires six months after the date it is signed.

[d] General Authorization. A general authorization for the disclosure of health-related information shall not be construed as written authorization pursuant to informed consent for the disclosure of protected health information unless such authorization also complies with this Section.

[e] Inability to Provide Informed Consent. When the individual who is the subject of protected health information is not competent or is otherwise legally unable to give informed consent for the disclosure of protected health information, written authorization under Subsection [a] may be provided by the individual's parents, legal guardians, or other persons lawfully authorized to make health care decisions for the individual. For the purposes of this Subsection, a minor under the age of [to be inserted consistent with state law] years is unable to give informed consent.

Section 4-103. Scope of Disclosures

[a] Generally. Protected health information shall be disclosed with the informed consent of the individual who is the subject of the information to any person and for any purpose for which the disclosure is authorized pursuant to informed consent.

[b] Non-identifiable Information. Any disclosures of protected health information permitted by this Act shall be disclosed in a non-identifiable form whenever possible, consistent with the accomplishment of legitimate public health purposes, except when the disclosure is authorized through the informed consent of the individual who is the subject of the information.

[c] Minimum Information. Any disclosures of protected health information permitted by this Act shall be limited to the minimum amount of information which the person making the disclosure reasonably believes is necessary to accomplish the purpose of the disclosure, except when the disclosure is authorized through the informed consent of the individual who is the subject of the information.

[d] Accompanying Statement. Whenever disclosure of protected health information is made pursuant to this Act, such disclosures shall be accompanied or followed by [in cases of oral disclosures, within three days] a statement in writing concerning the public health agency's disclosure policy, which shall include the following or substantially similar language: "This information has been disclosed to you from confidential public health records protected by state and federal law. Any further disclosure of this information in an identifiable form may be prohibited without the written informed consent of the person who is the subject of the information or as otherwise permitted by federal or state law. Unauthorized disclosure of this information may result in significant criminal or civil penalties, including imprisonment and monetary damages."

Section 4-104. Disclosures Without Informed Consent

Protected health information may be disclosed without the informed consent of the individual who is the subject of the information where such disclosures:

[a] are made directly to the individual;

[b] are made to appropriate federal agencies or authorities as required by federal or State law; or

[c] are made to health care personnel to the extent necessary in a medical emergency to protect the health or life of the person who is the subject of the information from serious, imminent harm.

Section 4-105. Disclosures for Criminal or Civil Purposes

No protected health information shall be disclosed, discoverable, or compelled to be produced pursuant to subpoena, compelled testimony of public health officials or other persons who have knowledge of such information subsequent to its acquisition by the public health agency, in any civil, criminal, administrative, or other legal proceeding, except:

[a] Court Order. A public health agency or authorized public health official may seek a court order granting the disclosure of protected health information upon an application showing a clear danger to an individual or the public health that can only be averted or mitigated through a disclosure by the public health agency.

[b] Sealed Records and In Camera Proceedings. Upon receiving an application for an order authorizing disclosure pursuant to this Section, the court shall enter an order directing that all materials which are part of the application and decision of the court be sealed. Such materials shall not be made available to any person except to the ex-

tent necessary to conduct proceedings concerning the application, including any appeal. Such order shall further direct that all proceedings concerning the application be conducted in camera.

[c] Notification. Any individual about whom protected health information is sought and any person holding protected health information from whom disclosure is sought shall be notified of an application for its disclosure pursuant to this Section.

[d] Response or Appearance. Any individual about whom protected health information is sought and any person holding protected health information from whom disclosure is sought may file a written response to the application, or appear in person for the limited purpose of providing evidence on the statutory criteria for the issuance of an order pursuant to this Section. The court may grant an order without such notice or appearance where an application by a public health agency or authorized public health official requires immediate action to avert or mitigate a clear danger to the public health.

[e] Findings of Fact. In assessing clear danger under this Section, the court shall provide written findings of fact and shall weigh the need for disclosure against the privacy interests of the individual who is the subject of the protected health information and any legitimate public health purpose which may be curtailed by disclosure.

[f] Authorizing Order. An order authorizing disclosure of protected health information shall:

(1) limit disclosure to that information which is necessary pursuant to the application;

(2) limit disclosure to those persons who need the information and specifically prohibit re-disclosure to any other persons;

(3) include any other measures which the court deems necessary to limit any disclosures not authorized by the order; and

(4) conform to the other provisions of this Act to the extent possible.

Section 4-106. Disclosures for Health Oversight Purposes

A public health agency may disclose protected health information to a health oversight agency to enable the agency to perform a health oversight function authorized by law if:

[a] the public health agency itself is the focus of the oversight inquiry;

[b] the protected health information is not removed from the premises, custody, or control of the public health agency; and

[c] the health oversight agency does not record the names or other identifying information of individuals who are the subjects of protected health information.

Section 4-107. Deceased Individuals

[a] Generally. Nothing in this Act shall prohibit the disclosure of protected health information:

(1) in a certificate of death, autopsy report, or related documents prepared under applicable laws or regulations;

(2) for the purposes of identifying a deceased individual;

(3) for the purposes of determining a deceased individual's manner of death by a chief medical examiner or the examiner's designee; or

(4) to provide necessary information about a deceased individual who is a donor or prospective donor of an anatomical gift.

[b] Deceased Rights. The rights of a deceased individual as provided by this Act may be exercised for a period of [two] years after the date of death by one of the individuals in the following order of priority, subject to any written limitations or restrictions by the decedent:

(1) an executor or administrator of the estate of a deceased individual, or one soon to be appointed in accordance with a will or other legal instrument;

(2) a surviving spouse or domestic partner;

(3) an adult child;

(4) a parent; or

(5) another person authorized by law to act for the individual decedent.

Section 4-108. Secondary Disclosures

No person to whom protected health information has been disclosed pursuant to this Act shall disclose the information to another person except as authorized by this Act. This Section shall not apply to:

[a] the individual who is the subject of the information;

[b] the individual's parents, legal guardians, or other persons lawfully authorized to make health care decisions for the individual

where the individual who is the subject of the information is unable to give legal consent under Section 4-102; or

[c] any person who is specifically required by federal or state law to disclose the information.

Section 4-109. Record of Disclosures

[a] Generally. A public health agency shall establish a written or electronic record of any of its disclosures of protected health information authorized by this Act. This record shall be treated as protected health information for the purposes of this Act.

[b] Information Recorded. The record of disclosures shall include the following information:

(1) the name, title, address, and institutional affiliation, if any, of the person to whom protected health information is disclosed;

(2) the date and purpose of the disclosure;

(3) a brief description of the information disclosed; and

(4) the legal authority for the disclosure.

[c] Maintenance. This record shall be maintained by the public health agency for a period of ten years, even if the protected health information disclosed is no longer in the agency's possession.

ARTICLE V: SECURITY SAFEGUARDS AND RECORD RETENTION

Section 5-101. Duty to Hold Information Secure

[a] Generally. Public health agencies have a duty to acquire, use, disclose, and store protected health information in a confidential manner which safeguards the security of the information.

[b] Security Measures. Public health agencies and other persons who are the recipients of protected health information disclosed by any agency, other than the individual (or the individual's lawful representative) who is the subject of the information, shall take appropriate measures to protect the security of such information, including:

(1) maintaining such information in a physically secure environment, including:

[i] minimizing the physical places in which such information is used or stored; and

[ii] prohibiting the use or storage of such information in places where the security of the information may likely be breached or is otherwise significantly threatened;

(2) maintaining such information in a technologically secure environment;

(3) identifying and limiting the persons having access to such information to those who have a demonstrable need to access such information;

(4) reducing the length of time that such information is used or stored in a personally-identifiable form to that period of time which is necessary for the use of the information;

(5) eliminating unnecessary physical or electronic transfers of such information;

(6) expunging duplicate, unnecessary copies of such information;

(7) developing and distributing written guidelines consistent with this Act concerning the preservation of the security of such information;

(8) assigning personal responsibility to persons who acquire, use, disclose, or store such information for preserving its security;

(9) providing initial and periodic security training of all persons who acquire, use, disclose, or store such information;

(10) thoroughly investigating any potential or actual breaches of security concerning such information;

(11) imposing disciplinary sanctions for any breaches of security when appropriate; and

(12) undertaking continuous review and assessment of security standards.

[c] Display of Written Protections. Wherever protected health information is made accessible to public health officials on the premises of a public health agency, there shall be prominently displayed a notice in writing concerning the agency's disclosure policy, which shall include the following or substantially similar language: "Protected health information contains health-related information about individuals which may be highly-sensitive. This information is entitled to significant privacy protections under federal and state law. The disclosure of this information outside public health agencies in an identifiable form is prohibited without the written consent of the person who is the subject of the information, unless specifically permitted by federal or state law.

Unauthorized disclosures of this information may result in significant criminal or civil penalties, including imprisonment and monetary damages."

[d] Individuals on Agency Premises. All public health officials or other persons having authority at any time to acquire, use, disclose, or store protected health information shall:

(1) be individually informed of their personal responsibility for preserving the security of protected health information;

(2) execute a confidentiality statement prior to entering the premises, or as soon thereafter as possible, pursuant to their review of written guidelines consistent with this Act concerning the preservation of the security of such information;

(3) fulfill their personal responsibility for preserving the security of protected health information to the degree possible; and

(4) report to the public health information officer any known security breaches or actions which may lead to security breaches.

[e] Individual Identity. The identity of any person making a report under Subsection [d](4) shall not be revealed, without the consent of the person making the report, to anyone other than investigating public health officials or law enforcement officers.

[f] CDC Security Guidelines for HIV/AIDS Data. Notwithstanding any other provisions of this Act, protected health information concerning HIV or AIDS shall be secured in accordance with written standards promulgated by the federal Centers for Disease Control and Prevention of the Department of Health and Human Services, as amended.

Section 5-102. Establishment of Public Health Information Officer

[a] Generally. Public health agencies shall appoint or designate a public health official as the agency's "public health information officer."

[b] Responsibilities. The public health information officer has overall responsibility for preserving the security of all protected health information consistent with this Section and the Act. This person shall report directly to the highest ranking public health official at the agency.

[c] Duties. The public health information officer shall perform all duties as required by this Section and the Act, including:

(1) monitoring the acquisition, use, disclosure, and storage of protected health information to ensure such activities are conducted in a physically and technologically secure environment;

(2) developing and implementing written policies and guidelines to preserve the security of protected health information, including a model confidentiality statement pursuant to Section 5-101[d](2);

(3) coordinating the assignment of personal responsibility to each person who acquires, uses, discloses, or stores such information for preserving its security;

(4) acting as the agency's principal investigator for each investigation of any security breach;

(5) recommending disciplinary sanctions for any security breaches to the highest ranking public health official at the agency who shall be responsible for issuing and implementing any sanctions;

(6) coordinating with federal, state, or local authorities, where appropriate, in the investigation of any security breach; and

(7) preparing any report required pursuant to Section 5-103.

Section 5-103. Issuance of Public Reports

[a] Agency Security Report. Public health agencies shall prepare on an annual basis a report concerning the status of security protections of protected health information, which shall be distributed to the public health information officer for the [State public health agency]. The report shall be prepared in accordance with guidelines issued by the public health information officer for the [State public health agency].

[b] Comprehensive Security Report. The public health information officer for the [State public health agency] shall prepare a summary report on the status of security protections of protected health information for all public health agencies in the [State] within ninety days of the date in which reports required under this Section are requested. This report shall be issued to the [State Legislative Body] with any recommendations for amendments to the Act or other relevant state laws which may improve the security of protected health information.

[c] Report Information. Reports prepared under this Section shall not contain any protected health information. Reports prepared under this Section are public information.

ARTICLE VI: FAIR INFORMATION PRACTICES

Section 6-101. Individual Access to Protected Health Information

[a] Opportunity to Inspect. Within fourteen days of the receipt of a request to review protected health information, a public health agency

shall provide the requestor an opportunity during regular business hours to inspect copies of such information in the possession of the public health agency which concerns or relates to the requestor.

[b] Copies Furnished. Within ten days of the receipt of a request for copies of a requestor's protected health information, a public health agency shall provide without charge copies of protected health information in the possession of the agency which the requestor is authorized to inspect pursuant to this Section.

[c] Explanations. Upon request, the public health agency shall provide an explanation of any code, abbreviation, notation, or other marks appearing in the protected health information. A public health agency is not responsible for producing or reformulating protected health information, solely for the purposes of clarification, in other than its original form.

Section 6-102. Limitations Concerning Individual Access to Protected Health Information

[a] Reasonable Limitations. Reasonable limitations may be placed on the time, place, and frequency of any inspection and copying requests. A public health agency may ask to review the protected health information with the requestor upon inspection, although such review shall not be a prerequisite to providing the information.

[b] Information Related to Other Persons. Any information contained in the protected health information of the requestor that relates to the health status or other confidential information of other persons shall be deleted for the purposes of inspection and copying.

[c] Unrelated Information. Any information contained in the protected health information of the requestor that is not related to the requestor's health status may be deleted for the purposes of inspection and copying.

[d] Withholding Information. A public health agency may deny a requestor the opportunity to inspect protected health information in the possession of the agency or may deny a request for copies of such information if:

(1) the public health agency can show via clear and convincing evidence that the review of the protected health information will cause substantial and identifiable harm to the requestor or others which outweighs the requestor's right to access the information;

(2) a parent or legal guardian has requested access to protected health information concerning an individual over the age of [to be

inserted consistent with State law] who is the subject of the information and the individual objects to such access of the information within seven days of receipt of written notice of the request by the public health agency in possession of the information; or

(3) the information is compiled principally in anticipation of, or for use in, a legal proceeding.

[e] Request Denials. If a public health agency denies a request to inspect or copy protected health information, it shall notify the requestor in writing of the reasons for denying such request, including that the agency does not possess any protected health information which is subject to the request.

[f] Appeals. A requestor may appeal such decisions under administrative review procedures as promulgated by the [State public health agency] consistent with state or local law.

Section 6-103. Accuracy of Information

[a] Generally. Public health agencies shall reasonably ensure the accuracy and completeness of protected health information.

[b] Corrections. After inspection or review of copies of protected health information pursuant to Section 6-101, a requestor may request that the public health agency correct, amend, or delete erroneous, incomplete, or false information.

[c] Duty to Correct. The public health agency shall correct, amend, or delete erroneous, incomplete, or false information within fourteen days of a request provided that it determines that such modification is reasonably supported. The requestor has the burden of proving that information needs to be corrected, amended, or deleted.

[d] Written Notification. The requestor shall be notified in writing of any corrections, amendments, or deletions made, or, in the alternative, the reasons for denying any request in whole or part.

[e] Appeals. A requestor may appeal any decision of a public health agency denying a request to correct, amend, or delete erroneous, incomplete, or false information under administrative review procedures as promulgated by the [State public health agency] consistent with State or local law.

[f] Retention of Statement. A brief, written statement from the requestor challenging the veracity of the protected health information shall be retained by the public health agency for as long as the information is possessed. The public health agency shall make a notation of the disputed entries in the requestor's protected health information, including the

original language and the requestor's proposed change. This statement shall be provided to any person who is authorized to receive the protected health information.

[g] Subsequent Notifications. A public health agency shall take reasonable steps to notify all persons indicated by the requestor, or others for which known acquisitions or disclosures have previously been made, of corrections, amendments, or deletions made to protected health information.

Section 6-104. Appeals

[a] Generally. In the event that administrative appeals have been exhausted pursuant to Section 6-102[f] or Section 6-103[e], the requestor may appeal decisions of the public health agency in the State or local court having appropriate jurisdiction.

[b] Court Determination. The court shall determine whether there exists a reasonable basis for the action or decision of the public health agency pursuant to an in camera review of the relevant protected health information, the administrative record, and other admissible evidence.

[c] Relief. Individual relief is limited to a judgment requiring the public health agency to make available the requested information to the requestor for inspection or copying or to correct, amend, or delete erroneous, incomplete, or false information.

ARTICLE VII: CRIMINAL SANCTIONS AND CIVIL REMEDIES

Section 7-101. Criminal Penalties

[a] Public Health Officials Generally. Any public official who, knowing or in reckless disregard of the fact that protected health information is protected by this Act, intentionally acquires or uses such information in violation of this Act, or discloses such information to a person not lawfully entitled to receive it, is guilty of a felony. Upon conviction, the official is punishable by a fine not to exceed [$5,000] or imprisonment for a period not to exceed [three] years, or both.

[b] Unlawful Disclosures. Any person who, knowing or in reckless disregard of the fact that protected health information is protected from disclosure by this Act, intentionally discloses such information to a person or entity not lawfully entitled to receive it is guilty of a misdemeanor. Upon conviction, the person is punishable by a fine not to exceed [$5,000] or imprisonment for a period not to exceed one year, or both.

[c] Unlawful Access. Any person who by any unlawful means, including bribery, fraud, theft, false pretenses, or other misrepresentation of identity, purpose of use, or entitlement to information, inspects, copies, examines, or obtains protected health information in violation of this Act is guilty of a felony. Upon conviction, the person is punishable by a fine not to exceed [$50,000] or imprisonment for a period not to exceed [five] years, or both, for each offense.

[d] Commercial Gain or Malicious Harm. Any person who acts in violation of this Act under Subsections [a-c] of this Section for the purposes of commercial gain, or with intent to cause malicious harm, shall be guilty of a felony. Upon conviction, the person is punishable by a fine not to exceed [$50,000] or imprisonment for a period not to exceed [five] years, or both, for each offense.

[e] Enhanced Penalties. The maximum penalties described in Subsections [a-d] shall be doubled for every subsequent conviction of any person arising out of a violation or violations related to a set of circumstances that are different from those involved in the previous violation or set of related violations described in Subsections [a-d].

[f] Statute of Limitations. Any action under this Section is barred unless the action is commenced within [three] years after the cause of action accrues.

[g] Separate Offense. Each violation of this Act is a separate and actionable offense.

Section 7-102. Civil Enforcement

The [State Attorney General] or other appropriate State or local law enforcement official may maintain a civil action to enforce this Act. Relief may be ordered by the court as authorized in Section 7-103 of this Act.

Section 7-103. Civil Remedies

[a] Generally. Any person aggrieved by:

(1) the failure to impose and maintain adequate safeguards for the confidentiality and security of protected health information;

(2) the failure to supervise persons responsible for the acquisition, use, disclosure, or storage of protected health information;

(3) the disclosure of protected health information in violation of this Act; or

(4) any other violation of this Act, may maintain an action for relief as provided in this Section.

[b] Appropriate Relief. The court may order a public health agency, public health official, or other persons to comply with this Act and may order any other appropriate civil or equitable relief, including an injunction to prevent non-compliance.

[c] Compensatory and Punitive Damages. If the court determines that there is a violation of this Act, the aggrieved person is entitled to recover damages for losses sustained as a result of the violation. The measure of damages shall be the greater of the aggrieved person's actual damages, or liquidated damages of [$1,000] for each violation, provided that liquidated damages shall not exceed [$10,000] for any particular claim.

[d] Punitive Damages. If the court determines that there is a violation of this Act which results from wilful or grossly negligent conduct, the aggrieved person may recover punitive damages not to exceed [S10,000], exclusive of any other loss, for each violation from the offending party.

[e] Attorney Fees. If the aggrieved person prevails, the court may assess reasonable attorney's fees and all other expenses reasonably incurred in the litigation against the non-prevailing parties.

[f] Joint and Several Liability. Responsible parties are jointly and severally liable for any compensatory damages, attorney's fees, or other costs awarded.

[g] Statute of Limitations. Any action under this Section is barred unless the action is commenced within [one] year after the cause of action accrues or was or should reasonably have been discovered by the aggrieved person or the person's lawful representative.

[h] Separate Offense. Each violation of this Act is a separate and actionable offense.

[i] Pre-existing Remedies. Nothing in this Section limits or expands the right of an aggrieved person or the person's lawful representative to recover damages under any other applicable law.

Section 7-104. Immunities

[a] Disclosure Pursuant to Informed Consent. No person shall be subject to criminal sanction or civil liability under this Act as a result of disclosing protected health information pursuant to valid informed consent under Section 4-102.

[b] Supervisory Officers. No public health official who is a superior or supervisory officer over a public health official who violates any part of this Act shall be subject to civil remedies under this Act on the theory of vicarious liability, provided the superior or supervisory official:

(1) had no prior actual or constructive knowledge of the violation or actions leading to the violation; and

(2) was not otherwise directly responsible for ensuring against the occurrence of the violation.

[c] Absence of Accompanying Language with Disclosures. No person, other than a public health official, shall be subject to criminal sanction or civil liability as a result of disclosing protected health information in violation of this Act where the original disclosure of information was not accompanied by language required under Section 4-103[d]. This Subsection, however, shall not release from criminal sanction or civil liability the public health official or other person who failed to include such language in the prior disclosure.

[d] Parent or Guardian. No person who is the parent or legal guardian of a minor, or an individual's legally-appointed guardian, shall be subject to criminal sanction or civil liability under this Section as a result of disclosing protected health information which relates to the individual, provided such parent or guardian lawfully obtained such information in accordance with this Act.

7-105. Administrative Procedure Act Applicable

Any action of a public health agency made pursuant to this Act, including but not limited to public notice given, or determinations made, under Sections 2-101 and 3-101, concerning acquisition and use of protected health information, shall be governed by the State [Administrative Procedure Act (APA)]. The courts of this State shall have jurisdiction to review final agency actions in accordance with the APA, and may stay or permanently enjoin any such action that fails to comport with the requirements of the Model State Public Health Privacy Act.

ARTICLE VIII: MISCELLANEOUS PROVISIONS [OMITTED]

GLOSSARY

Acknowledgement—A formal declaration of one's signature before a notary public.

Active Euthanasia—The inducement of gentle death solely by means without which life would continue naturally.

Actuary—One who computes various insurance and property costs, and calculates the cost of life insurance risks and insurance premiums.

Administrator—The person appointed by the court to settle the estate of a deceased person if he or she dies intestate.

Advance Directives—Advance directives are verbal or written instructions made by you before an incapacitating illness or injury

Affidavit—A sworn or affirmed statement made in writing and signed; if sworn, it is notarized.

American Bar Association (ABA)—A national organization of lawyers and law students.

American Civil Liberties Union (ACLU)—A nationwide organization dedicated to the enforcement and preservation of rights and civil liberties guaranteed by the federal and state constitutions.

Attending Physician—The doctor who is the primary caregiver for a particular patient.

Attestation—The act of witnessing an instrument in writing at the request of the party making the same, and subscribing it as a witness.

Attorney In Fact—An attorney-in-fact is an agent or representative of another given authority to act in that person's name and place pursuant to a document called a "power of attorney."

Beneficiary—A person who is designated to receive property upon the death of another, such as the beneficiary of a life insurance policy, who receives the proceeds upon the death of the insured.

Bequest—Refers to a gift of personal property contained in a will.

Bill of Rights—The first eight amendments to the United States Constitution.

Capacity—Capacity is the legal qualification concerning the ability of one to understand the nature and effects of one's acts.

Cardiopulmonary Resuscitation (CPR)—CPR is a medical procedure used to restart a patient's heart and breathing when a patient suffers heart failure

Civil Rights Act of 1964—The federal act passed to provide stronger protection for rights guaranteed by the Constitution, such as voting rights.

Codicil—A document modifying an existing will which, in order to be valid, must be formally drafted and witnessed according to statutory requirements.

Coinsurance—The amount the insured may have to pay under their health plan for services after their health plan has paid its share—e.g., 10% or 20% of the amount the plan allows for the services received.

Conservator—A conservator is the court-appointed custodian of property belonging to a person determined to be unable to properly manage his or her property.

Constitution—The fundamental principles of law which frame a governmental system.

Constitutional Right—Refers to the individual liberties granted by the constitution of a state or the federal government.

Copayment—The amount the insured may have to pay each time they receive services under their health plan

Coroner—The public official whose responsibility it is to investigate the circumstances and causes of deaths which occur within his or her jurisdiction.

Decedent—A deceased person.

Decree—A decision or order of the court.

Deductible—An amount an insured person must pay before they are entitled to recover money from the insurer, in connection with a loss or expense covered by an insurance policy.

Discharge Plan— A plan which describes the arrangements for any health care services a patient may need after you leave the hospital.

Do-Not-Resuscitate (DNR) Order—A DNR Order instructs hospital medical staff not to try to revive the patient if their breathing or heartbeat has stopped.

Due Process Rights—All rights which are of such fundamental importance as to require compliance with due process standards of fairness and justice.

Durable Power of Attorney—Also known as a "health care proxy," refers to a document naming a person to make a medical decisions in the event that the individual becomes unable to make those decisions himself or herself.

Duress—Refers to the action of one person which compels another to do something he or she would not otherwise do.

Duty—The obligation, to which the law will give recognition and effect, to conform to a particular standard of conduct toward another.

Earned Income—Income which is gained through one's labor and services, as opposed to investment income.

Employee Retirement Income Security Act of 1974 (ERISA)—A federal statute which governs the administration of pension plans.

Euthanasia—The act of painlessly assisting in the death of persons suffering from terminal illness or other prolonged suffering. Literally means "good death" in Greek.

Execution—The performance of all acts necessary to render a written instrument complete, such as signing, sealing, acknowledging, and delivering the instrument.

Fiduciary—A fiduciary is a person having a legal duty, created by an undertaking, to act primarily for the benefit of another in matters connected with the undertaking.

Fixed Income—Income which is unchangeable.

Fraud—A false representation of a matter of fact, whether by words or by conduct, by false or misleading allegations, or by concealment of that which should have been disclosed, which deceives and is intended to deceive another, and thereby causes injury to that person.

Guardian—A person who is entrusted with the management of the property and/or person of another who is incapable, due to age or incapacity, to administer their own affairs.

Guardian Ad Litem—Person appointed by a court to represent a minor or incompetent for purpose of some litigation.

Illegal—Against the law.

Incapacity—Incapacity is a defense to breach of contract which refers to a lack of legal, physical or intellectual power to enter into a contract.

Incompetency—Lack of legal qualification or fitness to discharge a legally required duty or to handle one's own affairs; also refers to matters not admissible in evidence.

Indigent—A person who is financially destitute.

Informed Consent—The requirement that a patient be apprised of the nature and risks of a medical procedure before the physician can validly claim exemption from liability for battery, or from responsibility for medical complications.

Insurance—A contingency agreement, supported by consideration, whereby the insured receives a benefit, e.g. money, in the event the contingency occurs.

Legal Aid—A national organization established to provide legal services to those who are unable to afford private representation.

Legal Capacity—Referring to the legal capacity to sue, it is the requirement that a person bringing the lawsuit have a sound mind, be of lawful age, and be under no restraint or legal disability.

Life Expectancy—The period of time which a person is statistically expected to live, based on such factors as their present age and sex.

Life Insurance—A contract between an insured and an insurer whereby the insurer promises to pay a sum of money upon the death of the insured to his or her designated beneficiary, in return for the periodic payment of money, known as a premium.

Living Will—A declaration that states an individual's wishes concerning the use of extraordinary life support systems.

Long Term Care—The services provided at home or in an institutionalized setting to older persons who require medical or personal care for an extended period of time.

Medicaid—A federal program, financed by federal, state and local governments, intended to provide access to health care services for the poor.

Medical Malpractice—The failure of a physician to exercise that degree of skill and learning commonly applied under all the circumstances in the community by the average prudent reputable professional in the same field.

Medicare—A federal program, administered by the federal government, which pays part of the costs of medical services for people aged 65 or over or who are disabled.

Narcotics—Generic term for any drug which dulls the senses or induces sleep and which commonly becomes addictive after prolonged use.

Net Income—Gross income less deductions and exemptions.

Ombudsman—Under certain state laws, an individual licensed to oversee various health care issues.

Out-of-Pocket Maximum—Refers to the maximum amount an insured may have to pay in coinsurance payments for covered services under the plan each year before the plan begins paying the full amount of covered services.

Parens Patriae—Latin for "parent of his country." Refers to the role of the state as guardian of legally disabled individuals.

Party—Person having a direct interest in a legal matter, transaction or proceeding.

Peer Review Organization (PRO)—The agencies responsible for ongoing review of the inpatient hospital care provided to people who are eligible for Medicare.

Petition—A formal written request to a court which initiates a special proceeding.

Petitioner—In a special proceeding, one who commences a formal written application, requesting some action or relief, addressed to a court for determination.

Power of Attorney—A legal document authorizing another to act on one's behalf.

Statute—A law.

Suicide—The deliberate termination of one's existence.

Terminal Illness—An incurable condition caused by injury, disease or illness which, regardless of the application of life-sustaining procedures would, within reasonable medical judgment, produce death and where the application of life-sustaining procedures serve only to postpone the moment of death of the patient.

Unconstitutional—Refers to a statute which conflicts with the United States Constitution rendering it void.

Underwrite—In insurance law, it refers to the assumption of the risk of loss to the insured's person or property, by the insurer of the insurance policy.

Uniform Laws—Laws that have been approved by the Commissioners on Uniform State Laws, and which are proposed to all state legislatures for consideration and adoption.

Ward—A person over whom a guardian is appointed to manage his or her affairs.

Witness—One who testifies to what he has seen, heard, or otherwise observed.

BIBLIOGRAPHY AND ADDITIONAL READING

American Association of Retired Persons (AARP) (Date Visited: October 2002) <http://www.aarp.org/>.

The American Medical Association (Date Visited: October 2002) <http://www.ama-assn.org/>.

The Association for Responsible Medicine (Date Visited: October 2002) <http://www.a-r-m.org/>.

Black's Law Dictionary, Fifth Edition. St. Paul, MN: West Publishing Company, 1979.

Center for Medicare Advocacy (Date Visited: October 2002) <http://www.medicareadvocacy.org/>.

The Federation of State Medical Boards (Date Visited: October 2002) <http://www.fsmb.org/>.

Health Care Choices (Date Visited: October 2002) <http://www.healthcarechoices.org/>.

The Hospice Patient's Alliance (Date Visited: October 2002) <http://www.hospicepatients.org/>.

The Joint Commission on Accreditation of Healthcare Organizations (JCAHO) (Date Visited: October 2002) <http://www.jcaho.org.>.

The Medicare Rights Center (Date Visited: October 2002) <http://www.medicarerights.org/>.

Medicare and You. Baltimore, MD: U.S. Department of Health and Human Services, 1999.

U.S. Department of Health (Date Visited: October 2002) <http://www.dhhs.gov/>.

Social Security Administration (Date Visited: October 2002) <http://www.ssa.gov/>.

United States Department of Health and Human Services Office of Disability, Aging and Long-Term Care (Date Visited: October 2002) <http://aspe.os.dhhs.gov/daltcp/home>.

United States Department of Labor, Pension and Welfare Benefits Administration (Date Visited: October 2002) <http://www.dol.gov/dol/pwba>.